The God Who Heals

✦   ✦   ✦

The God Who Heals

Words of Hope for a Time of Sickness

✦ ✦ ✦

Johann Christoph Blumhardt
Christoph Friedrich Blumhardt

Edited by Charles E. Moore
Foreword by Rick Warren

Plough Publishing House

Published by Plough Publishing House
Walden, New York
Robertsbridge, England
Elsmore, Australia
www.plough.com

© 2016 by Plough Publishing House
All rights reserved.

ISBN (hardcover): 978-0-87486-747-3
ISBN (softcover): 978-0-87486-796-1

Unless otherwise noted, Scripture taken from the Holy Bible, New International Version. ©1973, 1978, 1984, 2011 by Biblica, Inc. Used by permission. All rights reserved worldwide.

Translated from the original German sources by Miriam Mathis

A catalog record for this book is available from the British Library.

Library of Congress Cataloging-in-Publication Data

Names: Blumhardt, Johann Christoph, 1805-1880, author. | Blumhardt, Christoph, 1842-1919, author.
Title: The God who heals : words of hope for a time of sickness / Johann Christoph Blumhardt, Christoph Friedrich Blumhardt ; foreword by Rick Warren.
Description: Walden : Plough Publishing House, 2016. | Originally published under title: Thy will be done : sickness, faith, and the God who heals : Rifton, NY : Plough Pub. House, c2011.
Identifiers: LCCN 2015048637 (print) | LCCN 2016002221 (ebook) | ISBN 9780874867473 (hardcover) | ISBN 9780874867480 (epub) | ISBN 9780874867497
(mobi) | ISBN 9780874867503 (pdf)
Subjects: LCSH: Consolation. | Healing--Religious aspects--Christianity--Meditations.
Classification: LCC BV4905.3 .B5813 2016 (print) | LCC BV4905.3 (ebook) | DDC 248.8/6--dc23
LC record available at http://lccn.loc.gov/2015048637

Come to me, all you who are weary and burdened, and I will give you rest. Take my yoke upon you and learn from me, for I am gentle and humble in heart, and you will find rest for your souls. For my yoke is easy and my burden is light.

Jesus of Nazareth
Matt. 11:28–30

Contents

God Hears

God Promises to Heal

See What God Can Do

The Hope That Is Ours

Foreword

by Rick Warren

AT SOME POINT IN LIFE, every person will experience suffering, pain, and eventually, death. It's inevitable. When it happens, how are we going to respond?

Many of us, even Christians, struggle with God's purpose when we are suddenly faced with a serious illness or terminal diagnosis. Our first response is to turn to God, asking him to spare us from the suffering. But what if his answer is not to heal us immediately but to perfect us through the suffering? Such a season can test our faith. But if we can surrender our will to his, through that pain God can deepen our faith, heal our soul, and restore our joy.

In their book, *The God Who Heals,* the Blumhardts remind us that physical healing is not God's greatest answer to prayer. True healing is trusting God even when we lack understanding. It's believing in the promises written in his Word, which renews our mind and lifts our spirit even as our body is failing. It's not giving in to our fears. It's about giving ourselves completely to Jesus. Whatever circumstance you are facing right now, this book of daily readings will help you focus on a closer relationship with Jesus, our one true spiritual healer.

When you go through deep valleys, God is there with you, walking alongside you as you experience suffering. He knows it well. He's been there. He understands. As one who knows great pain, Jesus is our Great Comforter. In his First Letter to the Corinthians, the apostle Paul tells us that just as God comforts us in our troubles, so too can we comfort others. How will you respond to the pain in your life? Our faith tells us that Jesus is the source of victory in our lives even in the midst of suffering. That's because God doesn't waste a hurt. He can use that pain to direct us in the way he wants us to go, to reveal what's inside of us, to perfect us, and to make us more like himself. He is the Great Physician who specializes in bringing blessing out of pain.

Open up your life completely to him and get to know Jesus more intimately. Soak in these "words of hope for a time of sickness" by the Blumhardts and find healing strength for your soul. Hide God's word in your heart, surrender your will, and trust in God's promises. He will carry you through to eternity. You have his Word on it!

Pastor Rick Warren
Founder, Saddleback Church

Introduction

by Charles E. Moore

MY FRIEND and fellow pastor, Richard Scott, had just been diagnosed with cancer when he addressed our congregation: "People facing serious illness or death must ask themselves: What am I going to do about it? Will you allow it to change you? Or will you resist and avoid God's will for your life?"

I have to admit those words bothered me. In what way did my friend need to change? He was one of the most humble and committed followers of Christ I knew. Besides, I had been taught that those battling serious illness needed to get well. Only then could they be of use to God, and to anyone else for that matter. They needed comfort, support, medical assistance. They needed life to get back to normal.

This was my first reaction. Yet deep down I knew that what Richard said was true. I had brushed against the stark reality of death before, when my wife was diagnosed with cancer at the age of forty. Everything stopped, everything changed. God was speaking to us, and we knew, though we never spoke about it, that her physical well-being was not the most important thing. Thankfully, through prayer, support from friends, and medical help, she recovered. But perhaps even more importantly, through this difficult experience God gave us a gift: something from above, something eternal, something lasting between and within us had become our main focus.

In our scientific age we are pounded with a different message – namely, that pain, sickness, and death are evils to be resisted at all costs. The marvels of modern medicine are trumpeted as the antidote to whatever might ail us, and there is almost always another available course of action, another treatment that holds promise. Even so, all of us have to contend with bodies that are frail and vulnerable to all kinds of disease, not to mention the inevitability of aging. And we know that having a healthy body is one thing; living a full and meaningful life, at peace with ourselves and others, is quite another.

There comes a time when each one of us has to face eternity. When this happens, our whole life is laid out before us. Richard experienced this when it became clear that his cancer was incurable. Yet despite his grim diagnosis, he lived as one who had experienced God's healing. Again and again he pointed me, and many others, to the freedom and peace that come when we confess our sins and can stand before God with a clear conscience. "Ultimately, healing is given when we repent," he once said. In his last days, he seemed more alive than ever before. He had embraced God's will, and was at peace.

How did Richard come to this place of acceptance and inner certainty? And where did he find strength to hold on to it as his disease progressed? During his last months on earth, he often turned to the reflections you now hold in your hands (which I was sending to him and his wife to read as I discovered them). Written by two men of deep faith who cared for countless suffering souls during their lifetimes, the selections in *The God Who Heals* can help us today to live more fully, and with more purpose, despite our suffering. They show us what we need most in times of sickness.

Who are the Blumhardts, whose words have helped so many people? Johann Christoph Blumhardt (1805–1880) was a pastor in Germany. Early in his life it was obvious that he was destined to be used by God. This can be seen in his ability to turn his childhood peers to faith and in his early work among hardened youth. Blumhardt took on a small parish in Möttlingen, a remote village near the Black Forest. Here he came face to face with the evil forces of sickness, addiction, mental illness, and other afflictions he could only ascribe to demon possession that bound some in his congregation. When the local physician asked Blumhardt who was going to care for his patients' souls, Blumhardt took up the challenge armed with prayer, patience, and persistence.

This spiritual battle began in earnest in 1841, for a young woman named Gottliebin Dittus who suffered recurring nervous disorders and various other strange and inexplicable "attacks." Blumhardt embarked on a two-year-long struggle that ended in victory over demonic powers. He never could have anticipated what happened next. Almost overnight, the town of Möttlingen was swept up in an unprecedented movement of repentance and renewal. Stolen property was returned, broken marriages restored, enemies reconciled, alcoholics cured, and sick people healed. An entire village experienced what life could be like when God was free to rule. Jesus was victor!

Word spread, and soon Blumhardt's parsonage could no longer accommodate all the people that streamed to it seeking healing. Eventually, because of restrictions placed on his work by church superiors, Blumhardt left his pastorate and moved his ministry to Bad Boll, a complex of large buildings that had been developed as a spa around a sulfur water spring. At Bad Boll, many desperate individuals burdened with mental, emotional, physical, and spiritual maladies quietly found healing and renewed faith.

Christoph Friedrich Blumhardt (1842–1919) was barely a year old when his father began his prayer battle for Gottlieben Dittus. Nevertheless, this experience would stand as a backdrop to everything he would experience in life. When his family moved to Bad Boll he was ten years old. Eventually, Christoph worked alongside his father, and after his father's death, he carried on his father's task.

Troubled by the publicity surrounding miraculous physical healing, Christoph retired from public preaching altogether. Although he continued to experience the healing powers of God, he came to believe that what the prophets and Jesus wanted most was a new world: the rulership of God over all things. God wanted to transform both the inner and the outer person, both individuals and entire societies.

No other writers have influenced my faith in God's goodness and in his healing power more than the Blumhardts have. With bold confidence in the God who works miracles and a childlike acceptance of God's will in all things, these two men point us to look beyond our physical condition to Jesus, who heals and brings life to both body and soul, and to his kingdom. For them, the redemptive reality of God's healing love not only comforts us in our affliction but has the power to renew our spirits, providing us with the peace that passes understanding. They assure us that even the most material remedies can be improved by means of prayer, and that when we completely surrender to God's will, much greater things will take place. This is good news indeed, especially for those who know firsthand the limitations of medical science and the impossibility of a pain-free life.

This is why I turn to the Blumhardts again and again to gain new courage and a fresh perspective. I've also shared their insights with friends and acquaintances who, in times of terrible suffering, felt bereft of faith and hope. Their words remind us that it is sometimes only through suffering that we come to understand and know the healing touch God wants to bestow. When we are confronted with our mortality, God wants to free us and show us that neither sickness nor death is the final power.

I trust that you, the reader, will find this book a comfort, but also a challenge to live more fully for God and more surrendered to his will. I also hope you will think of others who might benefit from reading it. Only in Jesus is there real and lasting help. He is the true healer, the one who will not only raise us up to eternal life, but who will restore all things. He alone can bring the abundance of God's unending life here into our earthly lives.

Turning to Jesus

✦   ✦   ✦

I

Here Is Good News

*Jesus went throughout Galilee, teaching in their syna-
gogues, proclaiming the good news of the kingdom, and
healing every disease and sickness among the people. News
about him spread all over Syria, and people brought to
him all who were ill with various diseases, those suffering
severe pain, the demon-possessed, those having seizures,
and the paralyzed; and he healed them.*

Matthew 4:23–24

THERE ARE TWO SIDES to the gospel of
Jesus Christ. It is a message of forgiveness of
sins, of everlasting life, but also a message of
opposition to human misery. Not only is an end to sin
proclaimed, but also an end to suffering and death. All
suffering shall cease! Just as sin is overcome through the
blood of Christ, so suffering will come to an end at the
resurrection. When Jesus performed signs and wonders,
he was proclaiming the gospel against suffering.

With this gospel we can be certain that the wretchedness of this world will cease, just as we are sure of everlasting life. We cannot separate these two sides of Christ. We must not one-sidedly emphasize the cross and forgiveness, while ignoring the resurrection and the overcoming of our misery. It is Satan's trick to try and make us waver so that the Savior does not receive a full and complete hearing.

Faced with the world's longing for redemption, it is obvious that we can never bring real comfort through the gospel as long as we stress only the one thing – that the Savior forgives our sins – and otherwise the world can go its own way. Similarly, we would be unable to bring real comfort through the gospel, if we represented the Savior only as a miracle-worker and proclaimed, "Be comforted, you can be healed through the Savior." Then repentance and forgiveness would be utterly forgotten, and no fundamental change would ever take place in men.

Jesus allowed the sick to come to him, just as he did sinners. He was ready to forgive sins and ready to heal. There were times when very few sinners came, only sick people. And Jesus welcomed them all. Oh, that the nations would hear the good news! That the sick would come, and that sinners would come – all are welcome!

Christoph Friedrich Blumhardt

2

Jesus Cares for You

Jesus left there and went along the Sea of Galilee. Then he went up on a mountainside and sat down. Great crowds came to him, bringing the lame, the blind, the crippled, the mute and many others, and laid them at his feet; and he healed them. The people were amazed when they saw the mute speaking, the crippled made well, the lame walking, and the blind seeing. And they praised the God of Israel. Matthew 15:29–31

GREAT CROWDS came to Jesus, bringing the lame, the maimed, the blind, the dumb and putting them at his feet; and he healed them. The news of his presence spread in a hurry. Indeed, if any one of us had been there and had heard of a chance to be freed from our affliction – who of us would not have given everything to come to Jesus?

Yet, it was not always easy for the sick to get to Jesus. Many relied on the help of others. These people must have had a lot of compassion and made considerable effort as well. How then could the Savior not receive them? Should he have shown less compassion just because they might have come to him for the wrong reason?

Compassion sees only the need of others; it omits all criticism and judging. Jesus never gave the sick a sermon first, or first examined their inner condition; he never asked them what sins they might have committed to merit this sickness. This would not only have been harsh but would have hurt the sick even more.

Why then are we so quick to judge the sick, examining them to find out whether they are remorseful enough or worth praying for? Jesus said, "Whoever comes to me, I will not reject." This is why it is always wrong to think that illness is "a blessing in disguise." What is more beneficial for us – sickness or health? The Savior certainly did not think that the sick were better off than the healthy, otherwise he would not have healed or bid his disciples to heal the sick.

Yes, God knows why some have to suffer; surely he chooses what is best for them. But the Savior welcomes each one who comes to him with deep compassion, and quickly the blind see, the mute speak, and the lame receive full use of their limbs. Let us remember this. All those who came and all those who brought the sick and lame to Jesus had a great deal of faith and hope. A lot more than we have. And in his boundless mercy Jesus healed them all.

Johann Christoph Blumhardt

3

All Are Welcome

And the power of the Lord was with Jesus to heal the sick.
Luke 5:17

WHEREVER JESUS WALKED or stood, power streamed out from him, healing and reviving both soul and body. Whoever came to him with a trusting heart found help. The Lord of heaven, the God of Israel – the strength of this God streamed out from Jesus and worked healing. How wonderful that God's Son appeared in this way!

It can hardly be grasped that God would draw so close to us with such kindness. How obvious it was that everything was rotten. How little fear of God there was on the earth. How hypocritical was the piety of those who pretended to be devout. Even the temple was made into a "robbers' den," turned into a marketplace.

Yet, he came. And what was he like? He came not as one who judges but as one who was full of kindness, warmth, love, and mercy. Nobody needed to fear him. Everybody was allowed to come, everybody was allowed to have hope – the wretched, even sinners and tax collectors. They could all come. And all who came were healed and satisfied. Everybody could rejoice that God's ambassador in person had visited them.

Because the Lord was so kind and good to everyone who drew near him, it proved that he really came from God. Who could be greater? Can there be anything more wonderful than knowing that this man from Nazareth came from God? Can anyone else satisfy our deepest need? Can we imagine anyone coming from heaven greater, more majestic, or more glorious than he? Truly, he is the One. "We have seen his glory, the glory of the one and only Son, who came from the Father, full of grace and truth" (John 1:14).

Jesus is still the same Savior today. So there is hope for everyone – nobody needs to despair or doubt his patience and love. No matter who you are, you can come. But you have to come! Come in longing for grace and mercy. Then you will receive his goodness in abundance. Even in these troubled times you can know his mercy and that when the time is right, God will "wipe every tear from their eyes. There will be no more death or mourning or crying or pain, for the old order of things has passed away" (Rev. 21:4). Praise to him for such immeasurable hope!

Johann Christoph Blumhardt

4

Come as You Are

Jesus stepped into a boat, crossed over, and came to his own town. Some men brought to him a paralyzed man, lying on a mat. When Jesus saw their faith, he said to the man, "Take heart, son; your sins are forgiven."

At this, some of the teachers of the law said to themselves, "This fellow is blaspheming!"

Knowing their thoughts, Jesus said, "Why do you entertain evil thoughts in your hearts? Which is easier: to say, 'Your sins are forgiven,' or to say, 'Get up and walk'? But I want you to know that the Son of Man has authority on earth to forgive sins." So he said to the paralyzed man, "Get up, take your mat, and go home." Then the man got up and went home. When the crowd saw this, they were filled with awe; and they praised God, who had given such authority to man. Matthew 9:1–8

T H E   S T O R Y of the paralyzed man should remind us of our own situation, because we are all broken people. Even if we are not physically crippled, our whole being is broken by sin. Corrupt powers of decay gnaw at our souls and bit by bit at our bodies, either openly or in secret, whether we are aware of it or not. Our spirits are dragged down into the captivity of fleshly pursuits. Many of us can barely keep our heads above water. We have either wasted our lives or become dull to anything of a higher nature. Divine things elude us, and things of eternal value escape us.

It would behoove us not to wait until the power of death and corruption strikes us down, as it did with this paralyzed man. Jesus came to make it possible for each of us to recognize our wretched condition, and in this recognition we can be healed. But we must not hide the fact that we are hurting in some way or another. That we are all in misery is evident by the fact that we come running when genuine help arrives, or even imaginary help, or when any kind of help seems to be on the way. Everywhere, as soon as a facility is built for the sick and disabled, people come flocking. But all this human help pales in comparison to the power Jesus had. When he touched people, life-giving powers poured forth.

And now, you dear ones, let Jesus work. Let him use your affliction to drive you into the light. Don't hide what afflicts you. Indeed, through Jesus we may look even deeper and ask ourselves what really afflicts us in our innermost being. Through Christ, we can turn to the light as poor, weak, and wretched human beings, crippled many times over, both inwardly and outwardly.

Don't try to hide your need and cheerfully ignore it. Even if this is heroic, it does not bring help, nor does it bring praise to God. We should rather be like the paralyzed man and show ourselves as we really are. Let us not pretend to be strong, but instead recognize our misery and bring it out into the open before God. The Savior wants to reveal everything wrong in us so that we can be healed. Only then can those around us, like those around the paralyzed man, be filled with awe and praise for God.

✦   ✦   ✦

The paralyzed man came into Christ's presence. We can do the same, whether we do this on our own feet, dragging ourselves to him and approaching him ourselves, or whether others do us this service of love and bring us to him, perhaps without our really wanting it. Hundreds of powers are at work when the Savior shows up. What is wrong comes into the open and is revealed to the eye of God.

What a blessing it is to come under the eye of Christ, even the eye of his judgment. That is how the paralyzed man was before the Lord. He trembled and shook, but his trembling and shaking was more genuine than if he had stayed lying proudly in bed, letting himself be cared for and fooling all his friends with his sickness, as if he were only to be pitied and there was nothing to be set right.

When Jesus comes on the scene, the truth must come out. We must not demand human sympathy the whole time. Besides, in the end, we can hide nothing; the eye of Christ sees right through us and discerns our innermost being – all that is still dark and sinful.

Jesus is never soft on sin. No, the very opposite. He speaks a sharp word and sweeps his threshing floor. He separates the wheat from the chaff, judging the feelings and thoughts of the heart. His grace shatters our fleshly nature, where no cloak under which to hide our shame is permitted. God reveals his love but only when we come under the melting fire of the Savior. We need not fear this, for God's justice is a justice that makes everything right.

Even if we feel we are poor and miserable, all is not lost. If we are honest, there is nothing any of us can cling to. Even if this or that was right and good, let us admit that it was still not pure. What we need most is to start completely afresh and come, broken and needy, before the judging presence of Jesus. We have nothing to boast of until he can live in us completely. Only then can we be healed.

Christoph Friedrich Blumhardt

5

He Carries Our Burdens

When evening came, many who were demon-possessed were brought to him, and he drove out the spirits with a word and healed all the sick. This was to fulfill what was spoken through the prophet Isaiah: "He took up our infirmities and bore our diseases."   Matthew 8:16–17

THE AMOUNT of need and suffering in the world, both in Jesus' day and our own, can hardly be overstated. The Savior not only healed all kinds of diseases, but also the demon-possessed. People came to him who were out of control and who caused their relatives an incredible amount of pain, since an alien spirit within them made them furious, raging, screaming, or unmanageable.

If this was the case then, just think how many so-called mentally ill and insane there are today. Yet hardly anyone dares to call them possessed. Still, one cannot help thinking of Jesus' time, when many possessed came to him. There are thousands of people among us today who are sick in the same way.

Yet we read how Jesus ruled over the spirits that oppressed people. He drove them out by his word. All this, Matthew quotes from Isaiah, was to fulfill what was spoken by the prophet, "He took up our infirmities and bore our diseases."

The passage in Isaiah says literally: "Surely he took up our pain and bore our suffering" (Isa. 53:4). Isaiah speaks more of a freeing from sin, rather than from sickness and disease; yet it is significant that Matthew speaks also of disease, that the Lord's Servant wants to bear *all* our griefs. Jesus took away disease and sickness and in this way bore our infirmities. It is as if Jesus had made the diseases of the sick his own, representing the sick before his Father, who had given him the power to heal.

Something similar happens whenever we intercede for one another – we take the sickness of others on ourselves as though we were praying for ourselves. Intercession to God is genuine only when we feel very deeply for each other and share in each other's pain; that is, when we have real compassion.

Our vocation is to represent Jesus, who was full of mercy. Everything we do must be done in his name and by his Spirit. "Carry each other's burdens, and in this way you will fulfill the law of Christ" (Gal. 6:2). But we must be on guard, for whatever we do in our own strength, including intercession, has no value.

Ah, may the time come when we will fully have what Jesus promised and sealed with his blood: the power of God for salvation that heals all wounds, including those of the body. This is promised to all those who seek him.

Johann Christoph Blumhardt

6

Jesus Wants to Heal

When Jesus came down from the mountainside, large crowds followed him. A man with leprosy came and knelt before him and said, "Lord, if you are willing, you can make me clean."

Jesus reached out his hand and touched the man. "I am willing," he said. "Be clean!" Immediately he was cleansed of his leprosy.

Matthew 8:1–3

A LEPER COMES TO JESUS in great trust that he can help him, although leprosy was, at that time, the most incurable illness on earth. This really took some doing – it demanded a great deal. All human wisdom lies far below the simplicity of such a wretched man. This poor man, tormented and horribly disfigured, knew God's greatness and might. Whoever thinks of God in this way has come very near to him. We should be filled with holy reverence to see one of the most wretched among men standing before his God with such confidence.

"You can do it, if you are willing," says this man. Christ cannot possibly lack the power, this man thinks. He could not lack power, since he has come from God. Now everything depends on whether he wants to use it. "If you are willing" means "If you have pity, if you have a compassionate heart – and you must have compassion. You can do it, if you want to. What more is needed to help me?" Such a noble way of thinking cannot come to nothing.

"I want to," says the Lord. "Be cleansed!" Now look – where has the leprosy gone? It is no longer there; it has disappeared. When a man like that leper possesses such a childlike heart, God steps in. He wants to reveal himself so that everyone can trust in his greatness and might.

We must believe that the Lord can do anything if he wants to. Yet in the garden of Gethsemane, the Lord prayed, "Not my will, but your will be done." Even though Jesus knew he had to drink the cup of suffering, he nevertheless prayed to be spared. And then the angel strengthened him. Likewise, if we pray earnestly, it may be that an angel will quietly strengthen us so that we may bear whatever is laid on us. And, as is so often the case, the Lord may even provide more than what we need, beyond our expectation.

If we pray with unceasing, childlike faith, and if it is God's will, the Lord will let us see his glory revealed in deed and miracle. "If you are willing, you can do it" is the prayer of all those who fear him. And in his great wisdom, the Lord will say, "I am willing."

Johann Christoph Blumhardt

7

He Is Still Working

Jesus went around doing good and healing all who were
under the power of the devil, because God was with him.

Acts 10:38

J ESUS DID NOT USE or require any formalities
when people came to him for help. With one word
help was there. He also did not withdraw somewhere, in a high and mighty way, and wait for people to
come and ask for help. He went around and came to all
those who were miserable and desolate, those suffering
in body and soul, and called to them, "Come to me, all
you who are weary and burdened, and I will give you
rest" (Matt. 11:28). He offered himself as the Savior who
would help those whom no one else would help.

Has he changed any? Certainly not! He traveled
from place to place doing good and healing just so that
all subsequent generations could trust him, and so that
all who are miserable and afflicted might always know
where to turn for help. Jesus still does wonderful things,

"going around doing good and healing," even if it is in a more inconspicuous way. He draws close to anyone in need and pain so that we, too, might experience first-hand that he is the one who knows how to help us. Still today Jesus works good and heals. The question to us is: Will we come to him?

Johann Christoph Blumhardt

8

You Are Not Alone

For we do not have a high priest who is unable to empa-
thize with our weaknesses, but we have one who has been
tempted in every way, just as we are – yet he did not sin.
Let us then approach God's throne of grace with confi-
dence, so that we may receive mercy and find grace to help
us in our time of need. Hebrews 4:15–16

THERE ARE TIMES when life gets so hard that you feel unable to pray; you may even feel you no longer have any faith. It seems as if the Savior is far from you and that you no longer belong to the Savior, or that you never were on the right track to begin with. It's as if you were in hell, gripped with fear and a sense of being lost. You may even wish you had never been born. The pain is too great, the future too hopeless.

How I would love to direct you in such a way that all darkness is taken away from your soul! But such agony cannot be blown away with one stroke. For that, we have to wait for a time of grace. Yet, even now the Savior can give you much, but only if you become quiet and place your hope in him. If you remain childlike about your condition, you will not think that everything is lost – even when you hear discordant voices inside you. The Savior is there to comfort you. And if you are unable to become quiet, don't worry. The harm is not irreparable. Inability is not a sin. The Savior loves you, if only because of your sighs.

Remember, Jesus came into the flesh, into your very need, so that you may know that God is not indifferent to your suffering. You sigh and weep, you are miserable, you mourn for the Savior. That is all right, as long as you do it in the right way. The Savior did not say: "Blessed are those whose cause is right." He *did* say: "Blessed are the poor in spirit. Blessed are those who mourn" (Matt. 5:3–4). Believe it!

If you can't feel the Savior, then all the more believe in him. Those to whom God's love is nearest are precisely those who don't see and yet believe (John 20:29). The same is true of those who don't feel and yet believe. The enemy often wreaks havoc on our feelings; but he can't touch your faith. The devil cannot own your faith – unless you give in.

Sometimes you will feel that you have no faith, and yet deep down you still believe. Believe then in your faith. Things will get better. Christ is there, even if he is somewhat hidden. Don't even be afraid of hell – he is there too. Anyone who sighs and longs will not be lost. It is for our sake that the Lord reveals his glory. Remember, the Savior intercedes on our behalf (Rom. 8:34) and cannot help but intervene with his assistance if you have a longing in your heart.

Johann Christoph Blumhardt

9

Jesus Is Fighting for Us

Some people brought to Jesus a man who was deaf and could hardly talk, and they begged Jesus to place his hand on him.

After he took him aside, away from the crowd, Jesus put his fingers into the man's ears. Then he spit and touched the man's tongue. He looked up to heaven and with a deep sigh said to him, "Ephphatha!" (which means "Be opened!"). At this, the man's ears were opened, his tongue was loosened, and he began to speak plainly.

Mark 7:32–35

T HE SAVIOR STANDS in our midst as a fighter for us. He sighs and looks up to the Father in heaven, and then he calls loudly, "Ephphatha! Be opened!" Perhaps this man who came to Jesus was timid about coming to him. He certainly would have been anxious when the Savior took him aside and touched him – not really understanding why Jesus did this. But then suddenly, with "Ephphatha!"

his ears were opened and he could exclaim, "The news is true, Jesus is the Lord who can put an end to sin and suffering. I have experienced it. Praise and thanks be to God!"

Beloved, this "Ephphatha!" must be the conclusion of the history of our world. The Savior is even now busily at work, turning the gospel that we hear into deeds. But the Savior must also approach us personally, in secret, and in secret he must pray for us before his Father's throne. And finally the great "Ephphatha!" will come; it will shake the whole world.

For the time being everything is hidden. The greater Jesus' victories are, the more they take place in secret. The way this man was taken aside by the Savior is an example of how humankind as a whole will be taken aside by the Savior. Quietly, but with deep ardor, Jesus will bring humankind before his Father's throne.

So we who are God's priestly people must cast the sick at his feet. We must cry out to him, "Dear Savior, *you* are the Lord. We cannot bear it that so many people follow false gods, for we know that *you* alone are the Lord. So here we are. We will not leave you in peace, for you came to represent us before the heavenly Father in order to help us." This is how we must implore him. It is our task as the church.

Oh, you dear ones, I am often very sad when I see so many Christians who no longer bring people to the

Savior on account of their sins and their suffering. We must not allow the gates of heaven to close between sinners and the Savior. The gates must remain open for all who suffer, for all sick people. Were it not for this, I do not know whether I could believe the gospel.

Let this be firmly established within us; then we shall help toward the coming of "Ephphatha!" The greater our regard for the one who was crucified and rose from the dead, the greater will be the "Ephphatha!" in the final days – like when God said in the beginning, "Let there be light!" Yes, one day we shall hear, "Ephphatha! Be opened!"

Christoph Friedrich Blumhardt

Trusting Jesus

✦　✦　✦

10

When It's Time to Let Go

Now Abel kept flocks, and Cain worked the soil. In the
course of time Cain brought some of the fruits of the soil
as an offering to the Lord. And Abel also brought an
offering – fat portions from some of the firstborn of his
flock. The Lord looked with favor on Abel and his offering,
but on Cain and his offering he did not look with favor. So
Cain was very angry, and his face was downcast.

Genesis 4:2–5

WHEN WE PRAY we must make a sacrifice. We first have to surrender something.
That is the difference between Abel and Cain.
With his offering Abel gave himself and all he had –
fat portions. Cain, however, kept back something for
himself and expected something because of his offering.
There is a big difference between these two.

We can make an offering selfishly, or we can make
an offering in true surrender. We can also pray selfishly,
or we can pray in true surrender. Some people pray

thinking only of themselves, quietly wishing to get as much as they can from God. Others, however, do not think of themselves at all and long only that God takes possession of them. Again, there is a big, big difference.

There are times when life gets beyond our control and fear overtakes us. Like Cain, we shudder and pray and make offerings to God. However, we only do this to obtain speedy help for ourselves and rid ourselves of fear. We humble ourselves a little and cry out, "Dear God, help me!" But afterwards we are the same old person, living life as usual. Once again we have our house, our health, our money and possessions, and we can look after our own welfare pretty much by ourselves. Perhaps we still pray from time to time, giving thanks: "God is kind. Without him things would not be going so well for me." But all the while, we are filled with selfishness.

When we pray, *what* is offered or sacrificed is not so important. People in the Old Testament could offer a little dove or an ox; it was all the same. It did not matter to God whether much or little was brought to him. What mattered was whether it was brought selfishly or willingly. And whether we pray selfishly or in true surrender is still important today.

Let us beware. God does not want our prayers and offerings if they spring only from self-interest. If we don't burn for God and for his kingdom on earth, our religion is like inferior plaster – it falls down again.

Praying for all our little woes is of no use, it does nothing for God. It kills true prayer, as Abel was killed by Cain. Let us take warning. Everything depends on whether God has us completely. So offer your whole self to God – this is the only sacrifice that matters.

Christoph Friedrich Blumhardt

11

God's Will Is Best

Now listen, you who say, "Today or tomorrow we will go to this or that city, spend a year there, carry on business and make money." Why, you do not even know what will happen tomorrow. What is your life? You are a mist that appears for a little while and then vanishes. Instead, you ought to say, "If it is the Lord's will, we will live and do this or that." As it is, you boast in your arrogant schemes. All such boasting is evil. If anyone, then, knows the good they ought to do and doesn't do it, it is sin for them.

James 4:13–17

WE MUST NOT TELL GOD what to do. Even less should we persist in praying until the Lord finally hears us. Such "faith" is resistance or even defiance to the Lord. Even if we include the words, "if it is the Lord's will," in our prayers, it is a sham. If we are honest, we often include these words only because we know we are supposed to. But we don't really want God's will to happen.

When we pray for God's will to be done, we have to be inwardly and unconditionally prepared to accept this will. It is not right to constantly and expressly ask for our health, or someone else's health, to be restored, especially when conditions seem to steadily decline. To pray incessantly does not help anyone – especially not ourselves or others who are ill. It only increases our tension and restlessness, and hinders our spiritual life.

This doesn't mean we should just give up. God sometimes allows conditions to get worse (he knows why) before he finally provides help. What I mean is that we should become more quiet and resigned in our prayers for healing and health. It is God's will that matters. And true resignation and submission to God's will puts everything into his hands, so that his help, when it does arrive and however it comes, can come on God's terms, not ours.

It is also better not to speak too much of dying or not dying. Each of our lives is a mist. Here we must become even more quiet, and in silence wait for whatever the Lord has in mind. If death is knocking at the door, we should prepare our hearts for either life or death (Phil. 1:20–26). If someone you know is facing a similar situation, help them to let go and accept whatever God has in mind. None of us knows what tomorrow will bring anyway. We must make ready our hearts. Then all will be right. God gives his grace to the humble,

and those who are most humble and do the will of God
receive abundant grace indeed.

Johann Christoph Blumhardt

12

Why God Waits

The Lord longs to be gracious to you; therefore he will rise up to show you compassion. For the Lord is a God of justice. Blessed are all who wait for him! Isaiah 30:18

SOMETIMES IT SEEMS as if God no longer cares for us, as if he has forgotten his people. This is what the ancient Israelites thought and said. However much they cried for grace, no help seemed to appear, and their worst fate was imminent.

But the prophet Isaiah tells Israel that not only has God not ceased to be gracious, but he longs to be gracious to them. As much as they were impatient for his grace, he was (so to speak) impatient to be gracious – he was actually longing to be gracious. God was not indifferent toward them; for him it was a pain to have to wait until he could again reveal his grace to them.

What does this mean? If God is waiting to be gracious, there must be a reason why he is waiting, and that reason must lie with us. He sees something in us, something that is not right, something that impedes his grace. And so he has to wait until this impediment is removed. The Israelites readily sought false help elsewhere – from neighboring nations or from other gods. How then could God be gracious and help them? Yet God still longed to show mercy.

We in our unrest also try a thousand things, not realizing that by so doing we get farther and farther away from God. But God longs to bless us. He wants to have our entire heart and our undivided trust, so that he can be gracious to us. But when we don't give these to him, God has to wait; and we, too, have to wait in misery.

Ah, that we might not make the Lord wait any longer, so that he can bring his great help of which we are in such dire need! He is ready, he wants to be merciful to us.

O Lord, show us your mercy. Take away everything that hinders your grace and keeps you from being gracious to us! Amen.

Johann Christoph Blumhardt

13

Your Heart Is Safe in Him

My son, give me your heart and let your eyes delight in my ways.   Proverbs 23:26

WHAT DOES THE LORD ultimately want from us? Our hearts. To act or live a bit decently here and there, to feel good about our virtues and accomplishments, to stroll through life being looked up to – none of this is what the Lord wants. God wants your heart, yourself, your real self. What finally matters is that you love him who is merciful, and that he has your whole heart.

The heart that strives for the good looks to God. Such a heart is made happy by the miracle of his grace. God's grace is always given to a heart that seeks him, and when relief comes, your heart will be flooded with more love, and you will feel liberated from everything that binds you and keeps you from being genuine. You will be truly joyful – you will be able to freely give or withhold whatever is required by the Spirit. You will no longer feel the need to measure up to anything or anyone, because your love for God, to whom you belong, will make you stand firm. Your heart will beat for what is pleasing to God, and it will be pained by whatever is done against him.

Happy and secure is the one who has given his whole heart to God. How simple this is if we but look to Jesus, God's Son and our brother, whose pure heart reaches out to us.

If you don't give your heart to Jesus, you will eventually become puzzled over what life brings to you – especially when things go wrong or when you have to suffer. You will not be able to discern where God is leading you. And you will be tempted to murmur and complain and become bitter. You will not only see things from a human perspective, but you will risk falling into doubt and disbelief. All your goodness, all your spiritual striving will then amount to nothing.

God wants you to rejoice in his will, so accept it humbly and gratefully. When he possesses your heart, he will guide you, not by circumstances or by the whirling events that press against you, but by his word. You will know how to accept what God sends because you will have ceased to have a separate will or self-will of your own.

May you learn to give your love and your heart anew to God each day, so that his ways – even when they are rough – do not appear strange and unpleasing. Surrender your heart and let your eyes delight in his ways, no matter what else may or may not happen to you.

Johann Christoph Blumhardt

14

Choosing Freedom

Since, then, you have been raised with Christ, set your hearts on things above, where Christ is, seated at the right hand of God.   Colossians 3:1

WHEN OVERWHELMED by trouble, learn to free your heart. Even if you are suffering from the most dreadful illness, when you can hardly stand it anymore, even if you spend the whole day praying and sighing, free your heart. Chase your illness out of your heart. Set your heart on things above and see to it that God reigns in your heart. You can carry your sickness in a bundle on your back if you like, but it does not belong in your heart. Free your heart, I say. Cast out your misery from your heart, and bear your cross.

Let us not be impressed by sickness. For what is sickness anyway? If we live in an atmosphere of life, sickness is dispelled like a mist. We experience this, time and again, and so do doctors. Our mortal mists are not as dense as they seem at first sight. They dissolve. At some point they are there, then they disappear, and no one can tell where they came from or where they have gone.

So free your heart. Let your head be concerned with trifles, if you like, but God the Savior must be in your *heart.* Don't let yourself be so hounded by trivialities that you are of no use anymore. Scores of people are paralyzed because they allow so many little things, especially their aches and pains, to enter their hearts.

Keep yourself free so that even in the deepest suffering, in the most unhappy of circumstances, in short, in all situations, you can joyfully serve Christ. Let nothing cloud your heart, least of all yourself – thinking and worrying about yourself. Instead, sacrifice yourself anew to God with prayer and thanksgiving. In this way you will give God the glory on earth, and he will lift you above all that presses down upon you.

Christoph Friedrich Blumhardt

15

Take Up Your Cross

Whoever wants to be my disciple must deny themselves and take up their cross daily and follow me.   Luke 9:23

JESUS CAME to destroy all the works of the devil, and this is why we are called to fight against every kind of darkness, including sickness. But what does this fight entail? It does not mean we automatically pray for God to help our every need and sickness. Rather we need to direct ourselves to Christ's death first and recognize our own guilt for the sin and suffering in the world, including the sickness in our own bodies.

Our priority should be that God comes into his own right in our lives. In other words, we must do everything we can to fight against anything that seeks to exploit the grace and mercy of God, anything that turns Christ, our Savior, into our little servant. God is not duty bound toward us. It is we who must deny ourselves and take up our cross. It is *God's* glory we must serve, and we must be prepared to let everything go and become poor, so that Christ alone is exalted.

Let us leave behind any begging before God and instead seek how to do justice to his cause. Put your own needs aside and do honest works of repentance, and do so joyfully, without grumbling and lamenting. Let yourself be judged, turn your inner life around, and stop looking at yourself and your own need. Instead, sacrifice yourself for the kingdom of God. Become zealous for him, and God will not let your life be put to shame. You will find that your suffering and distress will disappear by themselves.

Christoph Friedrich Blumhardt

16

Help Is on the Way

Cast your cares on the Lord and he will sustain you; he will never let the righteous be shaken.   Psalm 55:22

W E W H O A R E R I D D E N with care, fearful and troubled, are to "cast our cares on the Lord." In other words, we are to fling them away, leave them to him, and let the Lord take care of them.

I realize that this isn't always easy to do – to leave everything to the Lord. We try and do this, but still remain burdened. Our cares still weigh us down. Somehow, we do not believe and trust enough, and do not know how to unburden ourselves. We pray but then act as though we had not prayed. We say, "Lord, Lord, take this burden upon yourself," yet we do not give up worrying, and then doubt whether God has heard our plea. We are halfhearted children who do not yet hold on to the One we do not see as though we saw him.

Imagine carrying a load so heavy that you can scarcely move under its weight. At last you find someone who takes it off you. How light and free you feel! That is how we should feel when we have surrendered something to God. God will help us – that is his trustworthy promise – but only if we like children give not only our cares but ourselves into his care. He is faithful and will not let us down. Even when he lets us go astray, even when he leads us on roundabout ways, even when darkness deepens around us, he takes care of us. He always leads us to the goal he has in mind for us.

Sometimes peace simply eludes us for a long time. But God will not allow us to be shaken. Help will come, and it always comes in time. So do not be afraid. Remain faithful and stand true before God. In this way you will not despair or grow faint-hearted. He who perseveres will, in the end, see how much God's delay was his gain.

Johann Christoph Blumhardt

17

Even in Hell, Jesus Is There

For Christ also suffered once for sins, the righteous for the unrighteous, to bring you to God. He was put to death in the body but made alive in the Spirit. After being made alive, he went and made proclamation to the imprisoned spirits. . . . For this is the reason the gospel was preached even to those who are now dead, so that they might be judged according to human standards in regard to the body, but live according to God in regard to the spirit.

1 Peter 3:18–19; 4:6

AFTER his death Jesus descended into hell, for even in hell he must have people who want to hear him. In every sickness, in every kind of darkness he must also have people who want to hear him. So there is nothing that cannot be healed, nothing that cannot be freed, no reason for us to give up hope.

If you let the Savior come into your situation no matter how difficult and troubling it is, then redemption will become reality in you and through you. It is much more important to pray, "Lord, take me into your hands, let me be under your rulership," than to live free of suffering. Whoever has this attitude can play a real part in God's kingdom.

Your suffering is not in vain if you have only God's kingdom in mind and are willing to share in Jesus' burden. Open the way, therefore, for him to enter into your very being, into your suffering, and serve him there. You will have to be completely involved in the fight, but then the Savior will come. You will have to let go of all half measures and root out whatever is your pseudo-God, your pseudo-help, your pseudo-hope, or your pseudo-joy. One hope, one joy, one faith, one love – that is our Father in heaven, with whom we want to be.

Don't assume you can take a little twig of faith, another of despair, a twig of joy and a little twig of sadness – and put them all together in a fine bouquet. There is nothing wholehearted about that. What God wants is a wholehearted "Hallelujah!" We must throw ourselves in, body and soul, and let our suffering be to the honor and glory of God.

Remember, you are a child of God. Remain true to who you are and what he has given you. If you hold on to this hope, then in the midst of the greatest misfortune and darkness, even in death, you will be given strength, comfort, and the final victory.

Christoph Friedrich Blumhardt

18

Our Best Help

I remain confident of this: I will see the goodness of the Lord in the land of the living. Wait for the Lord; be strong and take heart and wait for the Lord. Psalm 27:13–14

I KNOW OF NO PASSAGE in Scripture that obliges us to do everything in our power to prolong life. Even if there were such a passage, it would give us too much power vis-à-vis God, who after all is the only master over life and death. It would be as if we should somehow force life by our own power. What Scripture does tell us is to be patient and wait for the help of the Lord.

To try and do everything to save or prolong life seems almost rebellious. Besides, where are we to draw the line, if we are duty bound to always extend life? What about the coward or deserter in war? Would they be justified in sparing their own lives? Doctors are required to risk their lives and be ready to visit people with even the most contagious diseases. They would be in a real dilemma if they were obliged to preserve their own lives at all costs. Surely there is something far greater at stake than saving our own skins.

Of course, it is not wrong to consult physicians. We should let the physician do his job, even if caution is warranted. To reject physicians out of hand not only amounts to loveless harshness toward their profession, but reveals an exaggerated insistence on faith – that faith has to accomplish everything.

What is wrong is frantically using any and every means. Those who desperately try any means are at risk of falling under the criticism laid on King Asa (2 Chron. 16:12). If we are going to use medical help, then we should at least be sure that it will be truly beneficial. Only when we are confident of this, are we justified in trying our utmost. But to try everything – especially haphazardly – is almost a sin.

We know how most physicians are always ready to give advice. All of them promise results, even when they contradict each other. And if they do contradict each other, what are we supposed to do then? In fact, if we step back a bit and are honest, how reliable are man's outrageous treatments anyway? How can relying on them exhibit a devout attitude to God? I do not call this faith and trust. The Lord is the only true physician, and so even when we use means allowed by God, we should never give them too much importance, as if they bring the decisive help.

We are called to wait for the Lord. Again, this does not exclude making use of the good things God provides in his creation. But we are too used to depending on these things, and then we don't experience the goodness of the Lord. Because of our lack of faith, we no longer live in a time of miracles, as did the Apostles. We must *always* be open for what faith can do. But how is this possible if we go to the ends of the earth to find a cure; if we run from one doctor to the next; if we consult specialists who live hundreds of miles away, incurring exorbitant expenses; if we squander all kinds of time and energy; if even in the last hours of life extreme measures are employed?

The Lord retreats more and more when we try and find help in our own strength. But he who stays humbly in the circle assigned to him and uses the means at hand, be they great or small, in the faith that any real help can come only from above, such a person will fare best. He who trusts in God, who waits for him to work, will find that the Lord comes to him, and that his life will be truly preserved.

Therefore, wait for the Lord. Direct your heart's thoughts toward the coming time of salvation, and dare to pray for a foretaste of this time. Then you will surely find the best help.

Johann Christoph Blumhardt

19

Keep on Singing

Praise the Lord! How good it is to sing praises to our God, how pleasant and fitting to praise him!　　　Psalm 147:1

T O   P R A I S E   T H E   L O R D is good. Praise is pleasant and fitting, far better than complaining and losing heart. Listen well. It is good to sing praises. Praise is truly fitting, especially from people who do not have good fortune and who have much reason to be sad and distressed. How heart-moving it is to hear their praises. What about the rest of us?

Can we always sing praises? Why do we always first complain or worry or resist? Yes, there are things that make us sad and unhappy, which cause us tears and heartache, fear and anguish. I don't want to say that we should never weep, never grieve. But let us remember that even when we are in distress, we can exclaim, "God be praised!" We can always think of something joyful. There is always something worthy of praise.

However, to say a quick, almost thoughtless, "Praise the Lord" or "Thank God" is not enough. We have to think more deeply about what these words mean. There is always something we can hold onto that lifts us and others up. If we grasp this rightly, praise will even take away the heavy load of our distress. Then the atmosphere around us will be good, pleasant, and comforting for all those who reach out to us in our affliction – our togetherness will truly be refreshing and a joy.

To fret and wail, to behave as if in despair, causes only heartache. Oh, if only those of us who are downcast and unhappy would be able to praise the Lord! And remember, especially when God has given his grace and salvation to you, do not take his blessings for granted, as if God was obliged to let it always go well with you. Such an ungrateful attitude is hardhearted, and those around you will simply run away from you. No. Learn to praise God, at least when you have obvious reason to do so.

If we are able to tell everybody straight out and with a joyful heart that we praise God and thank him for all his goodness, if we represent and proclaim our kind and merciful God, then we will be a great comfort to many people. We will forget about our own cross and rejoice with those who praise God. Then we will be able to sing songs of praise from the bottom of our hearts. How good, how pleasant it is to praise the Lord!

Johann Christoph Blumhardt

God Hears

✦ ✦ ✦

20

No Matter What, Pray

Rejoice always, pray continually, give thanks in all circumstances; for this is God's will for you in Christ Jesus.   1 Thessalonians 5:16–18

PAUL does not consider here what we are to pray for; rather, we are commanded simply to pray, and to do so in all circumstances. Why then do we think so long and hard before we approach the Father? Why do we first try everything else that people suggest and go to all kinds of trouble before turning to God in prayer?

Can it be wrong to pray to the Savior when it is all right to be healed by men? Why should praying be considered a presumption when we are only doing what we have been commanded to do? Would it not be more presumptuous to resist a direct commandment of the Lord? Some fear that they might be freed from their present illness only to be smitten by a worse one. Does that mean the heavenly Father gives his children stones instead of bread, snakes instead of fish (Luke 11:12)? Others claim that suffering is necessary. True, but isn't it also important to experience the help of the Lord? Isn't help of more benefit for the heart than any suffering? Who has ever been converted through sheer pain?

Whatever the Lord wants – let us gladly accept what he gives us and bear what he does not want to take away. But let us pray. It is the Lord alone who must do the work. And he knows how much you can bear (1 Cor. 10:13). If he does not immediately answer your prayers, assume, as Paul learned, that his grace is sufficient for you. The main thing is to submit to the will of God. When you do this, it becomes easier, and gradually the Lord will lighten your burden.

Therefore, in a childlike spirit entrust everything to the Lord, so that he may do as he pleases. If you do this in *all* circumstances, you will find that this is the best way.

Johann Christoph Blumhardt

21

Become Like a Child

Ask and it will be given to you; seek and you will find; knock and the door will be opened to you. For everyone who asks receives; the one who seeks finds; and to the one who knocks, the door will be opened.

Which of you, if your son asks for bread, will give him a stone? Or if he asks for a fish, will give him a snake? If you, then, though you are evil, know how to give good gifts to your children, how much more will your Father in heaven give good gifts to those who ask him.

Matthew 7:7–11

SOME PEOPLE, including Christians, believe that we have no need for miracles. But then we might as well forgo the kingdom of God altogether. If God can no longer prevail on this earth, if God no longer has any power in our daily lives, if the only thing that counts is our own knowledge and effort, then we may as well forget about the kingdom of God.

If I am no longer able to live in the relationship of a child to my heavenly Father, leaving the circumstances of my life in his hands – when I have to run around to all kinds of people, saying, "Help me!" – then God does not rule on earth. If the church is no longer able to pray simply, like a child asking his father for something, then God's kingdom amounts to nothing. The rulership of God gives rise to practical deeds on earth. And, God be praised, it is our task to demonstrate God's rulership and witness to it.

So let us leave our concerns and worries behind and embark confidently on doing God's will. Then we can feel assured that wherever Jesus is, that's where we belong. No one needs to have doubts. Just move forward like a trusting child. If you know that you belong to Jesus, then dare something. Entrust everything to God's care, and you will discover that something new, something fresh begins to take shape in you.

Do not try and take control, but like a child come to the Father – then you will notice the wonders, healings, and blessings that are happening all around you. Then you will be vigorous when the way is clear. Don't try and busy yourself with all kinds of remedies and solutions in advance, so that God has to follow behind to patch up the holes you have made. No, look for what God is doing, and once you see the way, step out onto it.

Christoph Friedrich Blumhardt

22

Facing Doubts

The apostles said to the Lord, "Increase our faith!"

Luke 17:5

WHEN OUR FAITH is insufficient, we must ask for what we lack. We must, like the father of the boy who was possessed, cry out, "I do believe; help me overcome my unbelief!" (Mark 9:24). And yet, the request for more faith is not enough. Whoever wishes to pray for more faith must let his soul be made ready for it. He must turn aside from anything that interferes with the power of faith. He must compose himself, gather his thoughts, his spirit, and all his faculties. He must also be united in spirit with his own people and must not be inwardly ravaged and torn. Then the prayer that faith may come will be effective. Faith will be given from above and will find a doorway by which it can enter the heart.

In this passage the disciples had been given power to drive out unclean spirits, heal the sick, and perform many deeds in the name of the Lord. They needed gifts in order to do this, and although they had accomplished many things, there were times and moments when they lacked these gifts – that is, they were not sure that something would really happen when they called on the name of Jesus. For this reason they asked the Lord, "Increase our faith so that we will have the power we need when we speak in your name."

How do we apply this to ourselves? May we also pray for more faith? Perhaps. Perhaps not. The main thing is that when we pray for more faith, we should never do so simply for ourselves. When we pray for more faith, we are asking for something greater to be given to the church. That is our obligation and duty: "Increase the faith of the church, of the people of God, and especially of your servants, so they may again experience genuine apostolic faith!" This should be our prayer.

It is tragic that so few people in the church dare anything in faith, and when they do, they ask for so little. That is why so little happens that brings glory to the name of Jesus. Unless we have faith, everything is useless. We desperately need our hearts to be struck again because we need faith more than ever. Though we must leave it to the Lord to whom he gives this faith, our concern must be that miracles again take place in the church. For herein lies hidden the glory and power of Christ. So let us pray for more faith, but let us not pray only for ourselves.

Johann Christoph Blumhardt

23

Before You Ask

*And when you pray, do not keep on babbling like pagans,
for they think they will be heard because of their many
words. Do not be like them, for your Father knows what
you need before you ask him.*   Matthew 6:7–8

MANY PEOPLE THINK their prayers won't
work if they don't utter them clearly enough,
or fail to explain to God exactly what
they mean, or don't speak loudly enough to him with
sufficient earnestness. But when this happens, prayer
becomes so exaggerated that our Savior even forbids it.

Obviously Jesus does not want to discourage us from
praying. His point is that when we pray we must have a
sense of proportion. Once we have prayed, we must be
quiet. We need to be like the farmer who has sown his
seed. Help will come only when you are quiet in faith.
Also in your sickness or with other needs, learn to be
still and look to the kingdom of God.

We can share our needs with the Father in a few words, without making a fuss, and rest assured that God already knows what we need and what he will do to help us. We don't have to explain our requests in great detail to God, or try and make quite sure that he knows our needs. God knows about even the smallest matters and takes them straight into his heart. We can turn to him by glancing heavenward, with no words at all. We can do this even when we pray about something concrete and tangible, or about something that specifically troubles us. We may realize that what we thought we needed is actually not necessary and that we can find a way right in the midst of how things are now.

This doesn't mean that we just let things happen – as if everything will come of its own accord without our longing for it. Nor should we just cast a brief and hurried request at God's feet. When this happens, we too easily lose sight of God, assume that everything comes to us without his help, and we forget to thank him. Then we cease to have a believing heart and are consequently not true children of God.

Jesus said, "Before you ask him." Therefore we *do* need to make our requests known to him, otherwise many things will not be given that could have been given. It never displeases God when we come to him with our heartfelt requests. A real child asks for *everything,* knowing God has an ear for him. We should bring all our burdens and needs to him, for at the very least this helps to make us ever more aware that in all things God is the giver.

God always has our interests in mind. He carries our various needs with fatherly concern, eagerly waiting for us to come to him. He has not forgotten us. And when we feel tempted to think so, then all the more we should remember that he knows it all and cares for us. In fact, he knows much more about us and our needs than we do. Simple, childlike prayer is enough to move his heart, give you something out of the fullness of his compassion, and save you from all sorts of fear and trouble.

Johann Christoph Blumhardt

24

You Can Reach Him

A large crowd followed and pressed around him. And a woman was there who had been subject to bleeding for twelve years. She had suffered a great deal under the care of many doctors and had spent all she had, yet instead of getting better she grew worse. When she heard about Jesus, she came up behind him in the crowd and touched his cloak, because she thought, "If I just touch his clothes, I will be healed." Immediately her bleeding stopped and she felt in her body that she was freed from her suffering.

At once Jesus realized that power had gone out from him. He turned around in the crowd and asked, "Who touched my clothes?"

"You see the people crowding against you," his disciples answered, "and yet you can ask, 'Who touched me?'"

But Jesus kept looking around to see who had done it. Then the woman, knowing what had happened to her, came and fell at his feet and, trembling with fear, told him the whole truth. He said to her, "Daughter, your

*faith has healed you. Go in peace and be freed from your
suffering."*   Mark 5:24–34

A POOR WOMAN had suffered severely for twelve years, during which time she had consulted many physicians. These doctors caused her even more suffering, despite the fact that she spent everything she had on the physicians. Fortunately, at some point the woman heard about Jesus and came to him.

This suffering woman touched Jesus' cloak. He immediately felt a power go forth from him and was surprised and asked, "Who touched my clothes, or me?" Jesus' loving heart must have been moved; he wanted to reveal the faith shown by this simple act, the real faith of this woman. Jesus looked directly at her. Trembling with fear, she realized what had happened to her and came forward, falling at his feet. Suddenly, all shyness and reserve left her, and she told Jesus everything.

This incident shows how Jesus is one of us, really one of us – not someone we have to fear in awe of his divinity, but someone who out of love allows us to touch him. He does not stand above us, and yet in his infinite compassion he radiates his divine majesty and glory. Let us remember this. Our Savior is not far off.

The woman dared to touch Jesus' cloak without his knowledge. How many others must also have benefitted from the power of Jesus in this way. How many more must have come to him weak, short of breath, half sick, with all kinds of minor complaints, and gone home strengthened, refreshed, and healthy. They received healing not because Jesus was aware of their need but simply because he was their brother. We, too, can find healing when we gather together in true love with Jesus in our midst.

"Your faith has healed you," Jesus calls out to the woman. Yes, it was her faith. Look what faith can do, even in the lowliest! "Go in peace and be freed from your suffering," Jesus told her. How happy, how joyful, how blessed did this woman return to her home!

Let us not forget that through our faith in Jesus (when this faith is part of a life lived in him) we can experience something of this power. How blessed, how joyful we could be if we would but reach out and touch him, who is our brother! If only we had more faith, even in simple things. Then the hand of the Lord would be shown far more often. Oh, that we would turn more readily to our dear Savior!

Johann Christoph Blumhardt

25

Finding Joy in Suffering

Let us fix our eyes on Jesus, the pioneer and perfecter of faith. For the joy set before him he endured the cross. . . . Consider him who endured such opposition from sinners, so that you will not grow weary and lose heart.

Hebrews 12:2–3

YOU MAY FIND yourself terribly ill and at the same time battling difficult emotions or nervous conditions. You get confused easily and are overcome with great anguish and fear, with the result that your whole body grows weak and heavy. The more you strive for clarity, the more confused you seem to become. Everything seems to be slipping away from you, including feeling the Lord's presence.

When your spirit gets darkened like this, it is important to remain quiet and composed. You must not get overly anxious when this happens, even when you feel worse and worse physically. Remember, dark powers are always at work, trying to lead us into despair, away from our true destiny. None of us is ever completely immune from such attacks. But if you worry too much about them, you only make things worse.

Instead, ready yourself to be steadfast in night and darkness. Change the night into day by keeping your sights set on the Savior, who is the final victor – the first and the last. With Jesus, daylight always returns. Consider him who endured much more than you ever will. And when you know of someone else who is especially under attack, assure them of your intercession. This is always a big help.

As you pray, hope that the time will come when the great victor, the pioneer and perfecter of faith, will break through the night for all people. Then all the children of God will live in the light and be truly free. "So if the Son sets you free, you will be free indeed" (John 8:36) – it all depends on whether we love him fully. So be patient with joyful hope.

Johann Christoph Blumhardt

26

God Loves You

Those whom I love I rebuke and discipline.

Revelation 3:19

THE LORD disciplines those whom he loves. Therefore, when we have to suffer it is a mistake to think that God no longer loves us. Such thinking betrays the whims of our hearts and our self-love. What if a child being punished says to its mother, "I see now that you hate me and can't put up with me!" How foolish!

When things go wrong, if you become ill for instance, or if your prayers are not immediately answered, don't think that God has rejected you. Such a thought comes from the Evil One. If hardship befalls you, it is precisely because you mean something to the Savior. He loves you.

For this reason we must not torment ourselves with all kinds of accusations. For indeed, we can torture ourselves in an altogether unhealthy and exaggerated way about guilt and sin. Not every affliction is a punishment for sin. Like Paul, we may have a thorn in the flesh so that we don't become conceited. Recognizing your own smallness is also a sign that the Savior loves you. Like Job, you may still need to prove your steadfastness in faith. But this, too, is a sign of the Savior's love, that he considers you worthy – through you he wants to show the Evil One that there still are patient and faithful people here on earth, even when they have to endure a great deal of suffering.

Therefore, no matter what you have to suffer, never doubt God's love. And remember: A broken and contrite heart he will not despise (Ps. 51:17).

Johann Christoph Blumhardt

27

Guard My Life

Guard my life, for I am faithful to you; save your servant
who trusts in you. You are my God.   Psalm 86:2

DAVID CRIES OUT to God in great need.
Time and again we find ourselves crying out
to God. Matters can get so hopelessly entan-
gled that we are tempted to give up. How easy it is for
us to think that God does not know how to help. When
this happens, everything is lost, and we do not want to
pray anymore. That's when we give in to despair. But
everything depends on your believing and trusting
that God can do what seems to be impossible.

David put his trust in God, he thought of himself
as a "servant of the Lord" – he stood ready to serve the
One whose cause it was and who was able to accomplish it. Since David was a servant, it wasn't up to him.
He simply exclaimed: "I do not know what to do, I am
at my wit's end. But you, O Lord, you know how to take
care of it!"

We rarely act that way. We want to be our own masters. We want to manage everything by ourselves and on our own terms. We want to be in control, and when things don't go our way, we get angry and bitter. Because we fail to surrender all things to God, to his mercy and strength, everything gets turned upside down and we are brought to ruin. It's as if we would rather bang our heads against a wall than keep still and humbly pray: "O my God, please help me!"

David, the king, casts himself at God's feet. David, the servant, completely trusts God to accomplish what he himself is unable to do. He knows that with God everything is possible and that God listens to our prayers and cares about them. This is what we want to hold onto firmly, in faith. For we will indeed receive his help if, like David, we can exclaim: "Blessed are all who take refuge in him" (Ps. 2:12).

Johann Christoph Blumhardt

28

Honoring God with Our Lips

The Lord gave and the Lord has taken away; may the name of the Lord be praised.　　　Job 1:21

EVERYTHING Job owned was taken away from him, even his sons and daughters. And yet he was able to exclaim, "May the name of the Lord be praised!" It is hard to say whether Job fully understood what he was saying, but this word of praise shows how entirely submitted he was to God. In the end, this was enough for God. Satan was defeated at the very outset.

What can we learn from this? One thing for sure – the greater God's plans are, the more surprising, the more incomprehensible are the things that take place. If Job teaches us anything, he shows how important it is to have a childlike faith that when God hits hard he always has something tremendous and good in mind. Let us believe this, whether we understand it or not.

Dear friend, no matter what confronts you, the best thing is always to do the same as Job and praise God. Never think that God makes mistakes, or that he can't work in a certain way, or that he doesn't honor those who follow him faithfully. Beware! Whenever you begin to accuse God, you have already strayed from the path. You must be very careful not to fall any lower, lest you abandon God altogether. Just think how much we please Satan whenever we resent and resist God's will. Think how ashamed God himself must be because of us.

Don't forget that our faithfulness is always tested. We pass the test only if we give God the honor in *all things* and turn to him reverently and silently no matter what he does. When we do this, Satan is defeated and we are assured of victory.

Johann Christoph Blumhardt

29

God Knows

If you remain in me and my words remain in you, ask whatever you wish, and it will be done for you. This is to my Father's glory, that you bear much fruit, showing yourselves to be my disciples. John 15:7–8

GOD KNOWS why he does not always do what we ask for. But there are a thousand wishes for which we simply have no reason to think that they should come true. Paul wanted to get free of the angel of Satan, but the Lord said to him, *"My grace is sufficient for you"* (2 Cor. 12:7–9). We have to see ourselves as poor souls.

The promises about prayer are not given superficially. So even when God does not answer us, he still remains faithful and true to his promise. And he does answer prayer, but ultimately he wants to see fruits in those who pray. Only then will he receive honor for what he has done. Then the praise which we owe him – and which is so often lacking – will be given. Since we are allowed to ask for whatever we wish, our prayers should be focused on something higher, aiming at God's kingdom and its fulfillment.

In the end the Lord will, in some way or another, bring about everything we have asked him for. Everyone who asks is dear to him; for the one who comes to God stands closer to him than the one who does not ask. God considers every sincere prayer. But his answers are often different from what we expect. And yet how often he answers in such a way that we must marvel and adore.

Although so much is still lacking everywhere, let us wait patiently for the great time of grace that is to come; it will not fail to appear. Then God's mercy will unfold, so much so that we will all be changed. Therefore, keep on praying. The angels will carry your requests to the Father, and his reward will not fail to come.

Johann Christoph Blumhardt

30

Stand Firm

Stand firm, and you will win life. Luke 21:19

W HEN EVERYTHING is upside down, when darkness seems to be gaining the upper hand, and when we see no way out, remember: patience, patience, patience. Hope in the Lord, who can change everything, who can lead everything aright, and who will be victorious in the end.

If we cannot stand firm now, we will surely find it that much more difficult in the coming times of distress. Patience is the most useful "cure" for the inner and outer life. Therefore, don't despair, don't lose courage, even if all roads are blocked. Persevere, even if you have to go through extreme need. With confidence throw yourself into the Savior's arms, hold on to him, and keep on trusting and hoping that he will reveal his grace and mercy.

To have patient hope shows that you have faith. If your patience is not tested now and then, how will you ever know whether you possess true confidence or not? Submit to the Lord's discipline, and your faith will truly be vindicated.

Yes, many people appear to be very believing, but faith can grow strong only when we have to wrestle for patience. Conviction does not mean much if we do not have a trusting heart. In this way patience is the outer manifestation of faith. And if we are to be saved by faith, then we will have to learn to endure. Patient endurance and faithfulness always belong together (Rev. 13:10).

So let us stand firm and endure any hardship – persevering in all suffering and under any cross. Let us always take into account that tribulation has to come; it will not fail to appear. But let us also gain life by being armed with the power of perseverance so that we can stand firmly when tribulation comes. By standing firm you will surely win life.

Johann Christoph Blumhardt

31

Take Heart

*In this world you will have trouble. But take heart! I have
overcome the world.*   John 16:33

OUR STRONGEST, most natural desire is to
get free of suffering and sickness as quickly
as possible. We find ourselves constantly
praying, "Take this affliction away. Give us good days,
so that all may be well with us again!" But God cannot
always give us good days. In this world we will have
trouble, and more importantly, Jesus must have people
who help him carry the misery of the world, who do not
shrink from distress and suffering.

The Savior himself leads the way, carrying his cross
for the sake of God and his glory. God is glorified
when Jesus innocently bears the sins of the world – our
sins – and openly demonstrates in his own body how
poor and godforsaken we have all become, and how
much we are at the mercy of death and destruction.
For this reason the Savior does not shrink from crying

out, "My God, my God, why have you forsaken me?" (Matt. 27:46). This should become our greatest woe – that this rebellious world is also forsaken by God, but unlike Jesus, it goes its own way. The Savior sighs to God about this.

Are we moved by this? Who of us sighs to God? Who is pained by the harm we have done and continue to do to God and his cause? Yes, we sigh and pray, but don't we mostly sigh and pray just for ourselves and our own need? We have so little heart for God. But that is what should pain us. Our longing should be only to honor God, as the Savior did, and to do so in our suffering. Only if we are imbued with the suffering and death of the Savior and only if, like him, we feel within ourselves the sin and the need of the world, is this possible.

When we grieve for the world and place ourselves in God's hands, then we can truly act in faith. Such faith will bear fruit, not in the first place for us, but for God and his kingdom. Then God can work great miracles. And then, when it is time, we will also see what we have gained. *Christoph Friedrich Blumhardt*

God Promises to Heal

✦　✦　✦

32

When God Heals

In your majesty ride forth victoriously in the cause of truth, humility, and justice; let your right hand achieve awesome deeds. Psalm 45:4

WHEN GOD uses his straight-edge of truth and justice the earth crackles with miracles. God's miracles are always related to truth and justice. That is why his deeds are never strange happenings that puzzle us and make us wonder what they actually mean. There is always light, always meaning in God's miracles; they always possess moral value. Instead of begging for miracles, therefore, we should pray: "Dear God, please see to it that only truth and justice rule in our house, yes, and in our hearts – do not spare us but go right ahead." Then there will be no lack of miracles. What needs doing will be done.

When hard things confront us and we find ourselves in a dilemma, not knowing what to do, we must *not* tackle the problem where the difficulty crops up and try to remedy it there. No. We need to look behind it to see where something is wrong and pray that the Lord will set it right. We may discover something false, something we cannot do away with in our own strength. Only God can do it. Hold firm to this truth and you will find that your wounds will be healed, and what is outwardly wrong in your life will also fall away.

How much untruthfulness still lies hidden within us, how much self-delusion and conceit! On the surface things appear quite smooth. But physical affliction, in the end, is the result of perversity in our lives. This does not mean every trouble or every sickness is the direct result of sin. But suffering and sickness are connected to the whole. We are like a chain, and our common malady bears its fruits, just as do individual sins. Things would be different if we really lived according to truth and justice.

Everybody wants medical help, wants to be healed, but who is truly interested in God? We do not want to be truly cleansed. As for myself, I do not wish to see a single miracle happen to anyone if it does not result in an inner restoration.

✦　　✦　　✦

During my lifetime I have often been seriously sick, and each time the Lord wanted to speak to me just in the circumstances of my illness. The moment I could take hold of the pain with joy, thank the Lord for it, and allow rays of divine grace to flow, God's gifts and blessings fell steadily on me in faith. The pain lost ground quickly, I was able to concentrate on the Lord freely, I was happy and joyful, and the suffering passed like a cloud in front of the sun. In other words, over the years I have received inexpressible blessings from being sick. Many of the sick people who come through my house have had the same experience.

Several years ago I broke my hand. At the time I did not know it was broken, but the pain got so bad I had to go to bed. Once I became calm again, I laid my good hand over the bad one, and literally thanked the Lord for two whole hours, letting the power and blessings of God flow over. I thanked him for allowing me, alone and undisturbed, to accept his words of life and to center myself on him again. As I did this, I felt that my calling was being strengthened spiritually, and at the same time the pain I felt grew less and less. In those two hours I received more strength, more healing from God than words can ever express.

A few weeks later a surgeon came to our house. When he happened to see my hand, he commented that it had been broken in two places but had obviously healed as well as if it had been in a cast for four weeks. This convinced me all the more that during those two hours of prayer – in which I did nothing but thank God – the Lord himself healed my hand.

For almost thirty-four years now, this has been my attitude to sickness: take hold of it with joy and thankfulness. Each time I've been seriously sick, the Lord has taught me important things. I have learned that pain does not have to be a burden. Instead, it has taught me to be quiet, to still my soul, and to turn to the Lord and ask: "Lord, what do you want of me now?" And God always makes it clear what I must still let go of, what sin I must turn from, and how I must with my whole heart repent.

Christoph Friedrich Blumhardt

33

God Reaches Deep

Later Jesus found [the man he had healed] at the temple and said to him, "See, you are well again. Stop sinning or something worse may happen to you."   John 5:14

EVERY PERSON who suffers longs to be helped, but how many of us long for a new life? Our human needs must not blind us to the Savior; they must not rob us of seeing the great, new reality that God gives in Christ.

Of course, it is natural to be driven to the Savior by our problems, especially if we've exhausted all other solutions. Yet who of us runs to the Savior because of our sin? This should humble us. From the very beginning God intended to make us loathe our sin, not our pain. We should long to enter into a new world, to become free from the burdensome mantle of sin that now envelops us.

The Great Physician fights for our faith, not just for our health. Do you understand this? God performs miracles among us so we can be reborn, not just for the sake of one or two people, but for many. Miracles are – and I am tempted to use a strong expression – painful deeds for the Savior. For if they only make us happier in our earthly life then nothing has been gained.

We should think more deeply about this. Think about how burdened we are with frightful death and gross evil – all because of sin. And still we fail to devote our energies to get at the root of our need. Instead, we skim off the nearest misery from the surface of the distress of human life and bring this to the Savior. "Help me here, and then I will be happy again." As though that could help! As though that could make any difference to our human nature! Even if the Savior healed a hundred thousand sick people today, would that really help humankind? In ten, twenty, thirty years it would all be forgotten again, and everything would be right back where it was. Outer healing alone does not help us – God's power reaches to a much deeper level.

Oh, if only our eyes would be opened! If only we would see how with Jesus we can completely overcome the misery of the world through his name! Oh, that we would see that in him the great victory over the world of sin is won! If only we could forget our need in face of the misery of our sin and, with eyes of faith, trust the One who will forgive and free us – and the whole world – from all evil.

Christoph Friedrich Blumhardt

34

Renewal, Day by Day

Therefore we do not lose heart. Though outwardly we are wasting away, yet inwardly we are being renewed day by day.   2 Corinthians 4:16

W E SHOULD REJOICE whenever some-one gets well, especially after we have prayed for him. But our joy should not be because the person got well. There are many who must suffer sickness until the end of their lives, so why not this one? Rather, we should rejoice because we see that the Savior has done something for a particular person, that this person's heart has changed and is awakened with new longing.

I want to say to all who suffer: Yes, pray that the Savior takes things in hand – he wants you to have hope – but do not regard getting well as being so important. The Savior himself was sick. He said, "I was sick and you visited me." Have you ever thought about that? Have you ever thought that there must be sick people so the Savior can dwell in them?

I often feel weak, miserable, and ill – all I can do is drag myself around. Outwardly I feel like I am wasting away. Nevertheless I am kept going. Time and again I am given fresh manifestations of God's kindliness, deeds of God that renew me inwardly and enable me to carry on. The main thing is that Jesus is present in our sickness. And so, dear friends, see to it that Jesus is free to work in you. Your longing should be that Jesus works something in you, and even more importantly, that through you he reaches others.

Whenever we are attacked by sickness, our first prayer should *not* be, "Lord, heal me, I want to be healed!" but, "Lord Jesus, bring about whatever is according to your will. I will accept quietly in faith whatever you decide, just as it comes." Pray, lest evil should have the say, lest darkness hold sway. In all the pain and suffering that may befall you, even in the midst of death and the distress it brings, seek the Lord and the desires of his heart. This must be your deepest, most pressing request.

If you take this stand, you will experience something of the kingdom of God. You will know as you have never known before where your help comes from. You will grow so strong that you will be able to overcome every obstacle. Walls of Jericho will fall and mountains will be moved. No earthly power will impress you anymore, be it good or evil. The only thing that will fill your heart is what comes from above.

Christoph Friedrich Blumhardt

35

After You Are Healed

Now on his way to Jerusalem, Jesus traveled along the border between Samaria and Galilee. As he was going into a village, ten men who had leprosy met him. They stood at a distance and called out in a loud voice, "Jesus, Master, have pity on us!"

When he saw them, he said, "Go, show yourselves to the priests." And as they went, they were cleansed.

One of them, when he saw he was healed, came back, praising God in a loud voice. He threw himself at Jesus' feet and thanked him – and he was a Samaritan.

Jesus asked, "Were not all ten cleansed? Where are the other nine? Has no one returned to give praise to God except this foreigner?" Then he said to him, "Rise and go; your faith has made you well."　　　　Luke 17:11–19

MY FRIENDS, let me ask you. If you were one of the ten lepers, how would you feel if God said to you, "Be cleansed!" – and then you were cleansed. What if you were freed from sin and shame and felt new life within you. Would you rejoice? Or would you be ashamed? Would you deny God the chance to say to you, "Be healed from your suffering"? Would you refuse to let him make you well? And now I ask what if I, or someone else, were to say such things to you? Would you answer, "That's impossible, how can anyone hope in these kinds of things?"

Help from God is being given more often than we care to admit. But too many of us belong to the nine lepers, we are not the Samaritan who returned to praise God. We see things, even miraculous signs, but do not give God the honor. We hear things and still do not fall on our knees. We are too self-sufficient to say, "Lord, my God and Savior, you alone can help us."

Do you realize that Jesus can actually be right among us and at the same time be quietly pushed off to the side? We can experience something inwardly, even healing, and be joyful about it, but then we put it in our pockets and think no more about it. There seems to be something human in us that always fancies itself to be great and wise. And then the very thing we long for gets struck out of our hands. We drop just the thing we thirst for, out of fear of some human opinion or reaction. We might accept the Savior as the one who helps, but we're afraid to mention his name and remain silent.

If we do not have the courage to witness to what Jesus can do, then we can go to church as much as we like and have all the correct beliefs, but we will remain obstacles to God's work on earth. We can go on talking about the Savior as long as we like, but what good is it if he is not honored? We can be healed and yet die and perish in our sins. Only when we praise God before men will God enter our world. Then, as with the Samaritan, it can be said that our faith has made us well.

Christoph Friedrich Blumhardt

36

The Gift We Don't Want

The Lord has chastened me severely,
but he has not given me over to death.
Open for me the gates of the righteous;
I will enter and give thanks to the Lord.
This is the gate of the Lord
through which the righteous may enter.
I will give you thanks, for you answered me;
you have become my salvation.

Psalm 118:18–21

GOD CANNOT HELP US unless he first humbles us. Therefore David thanks God both for humbling him and for saving him. How can we expect any help from God, any special attention, any kind of healing, if our hearts are proud, if we have not allowed him to take us under his wings as poor sinners – knowing ourselves to be insignificant and needy?

Let's be honest: we don't deserve God's help. We stand accused because of the many things that have estranged us from him. God puts things right but does so by driving us into a corner, through all kinds of need and anxiety. He brings us low until we learn humbly to throw ourselves into his arms and stand penitently before him.

Each affliction that comes our way brings us low. It makes us feel we cannot stand on our own. Then we realize that we are in the hands of another – that we are not people who can live without the help of others. That's what we humans would so much like to be. When we are in trouble, we have to bend low and cry for help. Then God is able to help. That is why we should thank God every time we are humbled and brought low. When God humbles us, he intends to bless us. So let us be thankful. Let us bow low at once.

Johann Christoph Blumhardt

37

Inner Healing and More

Therefore, since Christ suffered in his body, arm your-
selves also with the same attitude, because whoever
suffers in the body is done with sin. As a result, they
do not live the rest of their earthly lives for evil human
desires, but rather for the will of God.   1 Peter 4:1–2

I F WE DESIRE HAPPINESS and health but
not conversion, we are on the wrong track. The gift
of healing will make no progress without repentance. Never will a divine gift of healing make itself
felt unless it is preceded by repentance, by a cry of,
"Lord, take away the curse under which we moan!" The
Savior is not interested in playing a game of making us
ill and then making us well again. If you are laid low,
repent – that is what you must seek.

Of course, nothing is wrong with wanting to get
well, but I ask, what are we going to do with our health
if we do not consider beforehand who we are and what
God wants us to be? Oh, how many afflictions could be

lifted if more attention were given to the *inner* side. The Lord Jesus is surely our helper and healer, but this ultimately applies to the soul. It is far better to be cleansed than to be healed, for in everything he does it is our *soul* that the Lord is after. If you let him have your heart, you will experience his goodness outwardly as well, for when sin is forgiven, healing follows on its own – everything else will come right.

May the Lord put everything on a different foundation among us. He will surely bring it about if we long for it in faith.

Johann Christoph Blumhardt

38

God Heals for Good

And we know that in all things God works for the good of
those who love him, who have been called according to his
purpose. Romans 8:28

WHEN I WORKED as a teacher in the
Mission House in Basel, I came down with
a high fever, and the doctor diagnosed
smallpox. The following night, although calm and
composed, I wrestled with the Lord, earnestly looking
upward. At one point after midnight, it seemed to me
that a hand stroked me from head to foot, and I suddenly felt well and free. Yet, I had been so weakened
that I had to stay in bed another week.

Right during that time I had to fight continuously
against hostile thoughts toward a woman who worked
in the house. She had always been good to me, but now
her flaws got on my nerves. My judgmental attitude
took away all earnestness in my prayers and robbed
me of serenity of mind. I became very upset and hated

myself for how I was. I prayed intensely that the Lord would take away these terrible thoughts and give me peace. But it did no good. It was as if I were living in a hell of evil thoughts.

Finally I resolved to be patient and inwardly let go. I would fight these thoughts no longer and simply trust God. It did not take long before all the bad thoughts were gone, and opposite ones took their place. I learned something very important in all this: It is not good to fight so much against yourself, it is better to leave behind your fleshly nature and not feed it.

There are times when because of illness something new comes. In all things God can work good. But let me also say that I know of no passage in Scripture that teaches us that sickness itself helps to free us from sin. In and of itself, sickness has no redeeming power. In fact, some of the worst sins can arise when one is terribly ill. All of us have known sick people who have become unbearable, driven by a harsh and merciless attitude. It is awful to see their self-love, spiritual pride, presumption, and overrating of self, a dogmatic mind, and exaggerated false piety. And then to see how much need and sadness this causes for those who look after them.

None of us is freed from sin because of suffering. And yet God often chooses illness to discipline his people, to turn them around. Right in the midst of physical illness, he often shows us his grace and turns us away from a life of sin. This much is certain, we must never presume that sickness itself facilitates the way to heaven. Sickness should turn us to God and direct us to the cross. Illness can be a good thing, but only if God is allowed to use it to conquer sin – for the good. For when his cross rules in our hearts, it can truly heal and free us and we no longer fall prey to sin.

Johann Christoph Blumhardt

39

The Greatest Thing of All

Seek first his kingdom and his righteousness, and all these things will be given to you as well.   Matthew 6:33

ILLNESS has often led me to seek greater quietness, to seek anew the way that God wants to lead me. People assume that after I get well, I will take up my activities again in the old way. But times and callings change, and we do not please God by clinging to the old customary ways. Instead, we must pay heed to the signs that show us new ways.

Now that I am sick, I need to step back, step away from my own personality. I believe the Savior himself will come even more into his own if I would but step back. I see this as a step forward in my relationship with those who are close to me. What must be foremost is the kingdom and rulership of God.

For my part, I now no longer feel it necessary to intercede in some special way for the health of others. I will still pray, but the most important thing I want to pray for is that something of God's kingdom breaks in. Our fellowship is not based on whether or not God heals us physically. No, we come together because we rejoice in the Savior and the unfolding of his kingdom. This is what we live for, and for this we are willing to give up everything. Whoever seeks God's kingdom first and foremost will receive everything he truly needs.

When we intercede for others, we should keep our eyes on the kingdom of God, in complete joy and trust, thinking not of ourselves but of the interests of Jesus Christ. We need to stop coming to God for help for merely outer needs. Again, our fellowship is far more important in God's eyes and far more precious than anything we might hope to gain through intercession (1 John 1:1–4). Healing is one thing, but what the Savior wants is to rule more freely among us.

Let us tremble, therefore, before what God wants to do. We need to prepare ourselves for anything, especially if God decides to take something from us. God often takes a path that is different from what we think of or hope for. Let us be quiet, especially in times of sickness, and then we will gain something coming directly from God that serves his kingdom.

Christoph Friedrich Blumhardt

See What God Can Do

✦ ✦ ✦

40

Our Miracle-Working Savior

Then Jesus touched their eyes and said, "According to your faith let it be done to you"; and their sight was restored. Jesus warned them sternly, "See that no one knows about this." But they went out and spread the news about him all over that region. Matthew 9:29–31

JESUS did not like it when people made a big to-do about his miracles. He always had something more in mind than the miracle itself. When Jesus performed a miracle, what mattered most to him was that it would arouse a deep, godly feeling. His acts of mercy were signs of something greater – something beyond the temporal. He touched the inner person.

Jesus ultimately wants followers – people who are gripped by him and brought face to face with truly divine feelings for God's kingdom. Yes, his miracles displayed more than the power of God, not with some earth-shattering phenomena, but with a certain kind of simplicity, a quality that could lead the soul deeper. They were so simple that they often happened before anyone was really aware of it. Indeed, sometimes nobody saw anything extraordinary take place. Yet Jesus, himself moved by compassion, awakened love in people – the same love that he had shown to them. All his words and deeds came straight from his heart and touched people's hearts, which in turn evoked praise and glory to God. In short, his healing hand made the glory and love of God visible to everyone.

In this way, Jesus had to be a miraculous Savior, who by the Lord's power furthered the redemption of all people and all creation. And Jesus is still our miraculous Savior. Without his mighty deeds he is nothing but a teacher. But we know him as our Lord. Oh, that this gospel might be fully lived and proclaimed!

◆　　◆　　◆

The greatest miracles of God are not those that happen to sick people. These are not so important. It is much more important that we see things happening to the healthy, that we see changes in people's lives and in the state of the world. What miracles, wrought by God, am I thinking about? For example, when guns are no longer fired in war. Do you think that is possible? Such a thought seems to make everybody chuckle. But did not miracles like this take place in Israel (Josh. 5:13–6:27)? Similar deeds are what we need today more than anything else, so that everything is taken completely out of our hands and put into the hands of the Living One. Of course, when something does come from God, it will come at the right time and in God's way. What we need is God's reality to enter again into our lives.

Johann Christoph Blumhardt

41

Be Still, God Is at Work

In repentance and rest is your salvation, in quietness and trust is your strength.   Isaiah 30:15

THE PROPHET ISAIAH spoke at a time when God's people were in great danger from invading enemies. One can imagine the tremendous unrest, turmoil, and confusion that came when they were prey to the murderous, vindictive, blood-thirsty, and predatory enemy.

In such desperate situations we naturally become restless to the point of insanity and cry out in fear. Yet Isaiah tells God's people to be quiet and calm, to have patience and hope. Those who learn to be trusting and unruffled in the midst of affliction will find their way and will be helped. Their eyes will be more open, their feelings more sober, and they will find a little opening where they can slip through, which they could not see as long as they restlessly stormed and raged in their agitation.

I once saw wasps in a vineyard. There were little white bottles hanging on the stalks, open above and covered with sugar or honey. The wasps, attracted by the sweetness, got lost and stuck in the bottle. Why? Because once inside, they got frantic as they kept trying to escape through the glass. They lost their heads, so to speak, and forgot about the opening above, where they could easily have found their way out. But not one could get out; they all perished inside the bottle. Then I thought, that's how we are in our restlessness. We bang our heads against the wall and do not see how our restless spirit makes us blind to what God is doing, and consequently, we lose our way with no one to blame but ourselves. An unpeaceful heart is in danger of losing everything.

By becoming still, says the prophet, we will be strong. A quiet spirit rises up and looks to God, from whom confidence and courage come. Then we can dare to think, "Even if I can't do such and such, God can." We are able to visualize anew who God is, what his plan is for humankind, and how he wants all people to be saved through Jesus Christ. Such thoughts will surely give us inner strength and courage, and through his Spirit, something of his understanding and peace.

Oh, what times still lie ahead of us when we will really need the words of the prophet! Let us lose no time in turning immediately to God in hope. He brings us help in many things, in everything, but we must become quiet to see God at work.

Johann Christoph Blumhardt

42

Always a Way Out

For you, Lord, have delivered me from death, my eyes from tears, my feet from stumbling. Psalm 116:8

DAVID HAD BEEN in deadly peril, almost doomed to death. And yet God delivered him. So he praises the Lord for keeping him from stumbling.

If we – in our need and distress – can't see a way out, our feet will most likely begin to stumble, and we will lose heart. We will be tempted to fall into despondency, despair, and murmuring against God, perhaps to the point of not believing in God and his promise. We may even fall into false and sinful ways, taking things into our own hands – then we will stumble for sure. That is very dangerous. If we do not hold out when our faith is tested, we risk teetering on the brink of eternal death.

But the Lord is kind and will not allow us to be tempted beyond our strength. Before we really stumble, he always provides a change, a way out. David himself experienced this. God snatched him out of every danger. And we, too, can experience this. To be sure, temptations and struggles will still come. But we will never lack help and comfort from our faithful God. The Lord's signs of help will give us times of rejoicing and peace again and again.

Johann Christoph Blumhardt

43

Signs and Wonders

Jesus performed many other signs in the presence of his disciples, which are not recorded in this book. But these are written that you may believe that Jesus is the Messiah, the Son of God, and that by believing you may have life in his name.　　　　　　　　　　John 20: 30–31

W HEN THE FATHER in heaven does something, we should be all eyes and ears. Yet today, whenever a miracle takes place, we wrap it up and put it in our pocket, we keep it to ourselves. For this reason there is no blessing on it, and those around us don't want to hear anything about it.

When we see a sign, no matter where or what kind, our whole being should be filled with praise to God. If we have faith that floods us with love and compassion for our world; if through the signs and wonders that God sends us, we learn to have patience with sinners, to practice gentleness with our friends and neighbors; if, instead of taking the experience to ourselves, we lay ourselves at the feet of the world and say, "I am your slave, your servant. I will serve and carry you"; if we are humble instead of great; if signs and wonders help us become true believers instead of pious ones – then good will triumph, and we will be able to call forth more signs and wonders. That is the will of the Father in heaven and is what should be the result of a sign.

I've seen whole families brought close to the Savior through a miracle, enabling Christ to do further things in them. But this needs to happen much, much more often. Every person who truly experiences a sign, for whom the Father in heaven does something good, should become a new person. They should truly believe, and then their whole being will be filled with divine things.

When it comes to healing, the most important thing is that something of God is revealed on this poor earth. Hold fast to this and never let go of it. If you have been healed by a miracle, but still continue to give yourself to earthly things, what has been gained? If you lie mortally ill and the Savior heals you and you take it for granted, thinking only of your family and your business, what good is it? Look up. Look up. There is your prize. When we experience signs and wonders, something must change in us.

Let us go to the Savior in our need and cry to him: "Lord, help us!" But we must also listen to him. And when we have been helped, then let us do the will of God. Let Jesus wrench us out of our earthly ways so that we may have life in his name.

Christoph Friedrich Blumhardt

44

God of the Impossible

Is anything too hard for the Lord? Genesis 18:14

ABRAHAM was to have a son, though both he and his wife Sarah were well on in years. But the Lord assured him: "Is anything too hard for the Lord?" A similar thing happened to Mary, two thousand years later. She, too, could not quite believe that she was to receive a son. Yet the angel told her, "For nothing is impossible with God" (Luke 1:37). Jesus himself said the same thing when he told his disciples that it was hard for a rich man to enter the kingdom of heaven. Dismayed, the disciples asked, "Who then can be saved?" Jesus answered, "With man this is impossible, but with God all things are possible" (Matt. 19:23–26).

Through his own deeds, Jesus demonstrated that nothing was impossible for God. He performed mighty deeds that were human impossibilities. In this way he gave our faith a completely new direction. He changed water into wine, multiplied a small amount of bread and fish while he gave thanks, awakened Lazarus from the dead. Sheer miracles, which so many of today's clear heads cannot grasp. But for those who believe, Jesus is showing us God's love and that he can do what seems to us impossible.

This certainty of faith ought to continue today. We need not expect such great miracles everywhere. But if necessary, God can do the impossible. This is the kind of God we serve, and he wants us to show it.

Just as God created heaven and earth out of nothing, so he can create something out of nothing now. He can still change water into wine, multiply bread, and raise the dead. Such is our God. His kingdom will not be complete until a great flock who believe that God can do even the impossible, comes into being again. God wants to do something that only he can do. And he will do it again, because only he can end all the sighing and groaning of creation.

Johann Christoph Blumhardt

45

Miracles Beyond Belief

While the man held on to Peter and John, all the people were astonished and came running to them in the place called Solomon's Colonnade. When Peter saw this, he said to them: "Fellow Israelites, why does this surprise you? Why do you stare at us as if by our own power or godliness we had made this man walk? The God of Abraham, Isaac, and Jacob, the God of our fathers, has glorified his servant Jesus." Acts 3:11–13

TOO FEW PEOPLE grasp how God can work and how he can set things in order here on earth. We see things only from a natural viewpoint. Our educated outlook prevents us from seeing miracles.

Despite our modern outlook, I believe there is hardly anyone who wouldn't be exceedingly happy, even if only in the secrecy of his own heart, if a miracle were to happen to him. He would not reject it, if he were suddenly to recover from an incurable illness. No, he would gladly exclaim, "It is a miracle that I am well again." That is how most people feel deep down. People everywhere thirst for a Savior who does precisely these things, which so-called modern medicine has little time for.

All of us know that there are certain situations where we find ourselves completely helpless, situations where all the powers known to man are of no help. That is why *faith* cannot be rooted out of our lives. It does not matter how much water our sophisticated world pours on the fire of faith, our yearning to believe breaks out somewhere or other. Faith bursts out even if we do not make an opening for it – especially *the* faith, which thirsts for signs of God beyond our expectations and understanding. If this thirst is not satisfied, people are driven with a remarkable and mysterious power to go out looking.

Think of the many pilgrims who travel to Trier [Germany] to see the holy cloak, which is said to possess wonderful powers. Dear friends – the impulse that moves thousands to go to Trier is basically the same impulse that moved the ten lepers to go to Jesus. Although the goal is not the same, the power which drives them all is the same – a thirst for something we cannot comprehend or see, but which we simply need.

One of the greatest tragedies we face today is that we no longer believe in miracles. Not miracles by means of uncanny powers or by science, but miracles that lead people to Jesus, miracles wrought by a true word of God. Do we believe that we can be liberated from illness and death? Do we believe that we can also be freed from the confusion inherent in our nature, from the sin and the follies of our hopes and ambitions? Do we believe this is possible? Or is it not possible, is it nothing but a lie?

Christoph Friedrich Blumhardt

God Is Good

Give thanks to the Lord Almighty, for the Lord is good;
his love endures forever. Jeremiah 33:11

I T W O U L D B E very small-minded of us to think
that God stood alone and all by himself, aloof
from the billions upon billions of human souls
here on earth. He is the Lord Almighty, the Lord of
hosts. He commands great regiments and sends forth
his servants to help us. He can call one to himself and
say, "You go to such and such a person," and to another,
"You go to that one," and so forth. He has servants for
each of us – however many he needs, there are more
than sufficient. He has servants enough so he can
arrange everything to gain the great victory.

He is gracious, and with his help we can always glean
something good from whatever faces us in life, even
when so much that is not good is also present. It is his
will to do good, and it is only our sin that hinders him.
Our human will, which asserts itself, is the greatest

sin. But it can and will be overcome. Even if God must allow this or that evil now, one day it will be different. Death and sickness will be overcome and done away with, since their right to exist lasts only as long as sin is present.

In the end, God will be ruler in and through and over all with his grace and his goodness. So we can pray, "Deliver us from evil," for this actually means, "Do good to us for evermore." We can hope for the Lord of hosts to deliver us from evil right now, and the more we pray in a childlike way, the more quickly will this deliverance come.

That we may pray like this, with the absolute assurance of being heard, is something so great that we must give thanks to the Lord Almighty. However much wrongness and adversity there may be, God's goodness wants to shine on us again and again, and one day will prevail. All the powers of the enemy are even now being crushed and broken. So we have no alternative but to thank the Lord Almighty, for he is good.

Johann Christoph Blumhardt

47

Miracles of Mercy

Jesus stepped into a boat, crossed over and came to his own town. Some men brought to him a paralyzed man, lying on a mat. When Jesus saw their faith, he said to the man, "Take heart, son; your sins are forgiven." . . . So he said to the paralyzed man, "Get up, take your mat and go home." Then the man got up and went home. When the crowd saw this, they were filled with awe; and they praised God, who had given such authority to man.

Matthew 9:1–8

THE FACT THAT JESUS healed the paralyzed man with a mere word should convince us that he also has the authority to forgive sins. He who is able to heal, forgives. This is why Jesus' miracles are both unique and significant.

We must remember that diseases, especially those which possess a demonic character, are the consequence of sin and rebellion. If our infirmities are to be eliminated, the curse of sin will have to be destroyed.

And it has been. God hears the prayers of sinners who are repentant and humble; he will help them overcome their suffering. A restoration of health that occurs in a more natural way is surely also a sign of God's love. God sheds his grace on everyone – he is kind to the ungrateful and wicked (Luke 6:35). But this does not mean that their sins are forgiven. God may rescue us from death, but sin can still remain.

Whenever Jesus healed, God himself was present – the power that created something out of nothing – and sin was destroyed. This is why the one to whom God comes close cannot possibly remain the same sinner as before. When God miraculously heals, at that very moment everything that divides us from God is cleared away. We are freed from sin and assured of God's grace.

This is why only those who have faith in Christ, those who recognize him as the Son of God, are able to receive grace and forgiveness. Where Jesus found no faith, he could not perform miracles (Matt.13:58; Mark 6:5–6). But whoever approached him with child-like faith was helped. Jesus said repeatedly, "Your faith has healed you."

Today healing and forgiveness do not necessarily coincide. We await the fullness of time when the Spirit will be poured out on all nations. Nevertheless, through Christ, the one who "bore the sins of the world," a new and everlasting way has been established. Jesus gave the authority to heal and to forgive sins to his disciples (John 20:21–23). His gift of grace – complete with powers from above – is now passed on to all who embrace his reconciling death. What mercy has God shown us! Even today we can experience healing and the forgiveness of sins. Let us rejoice and see what God can do.

Johann Christoph Blumhardt

48

The Day Is Almost Here

The night is nearly over; the day is almost here. So let us put aside the deeds of darkness and put on the armor of light.   Romans 13:12

T HE NIGHT is nearly over; the day is almost here. And yet, it does not look as if day is near. Our feet still walk in sin, our hands do not manage to do anything good. Around us there are thousands and thousands of people who are submerged in the mire of corruption. They die in masses. There appears to be no day on the earth. But our faith demands it, our love to God, our hope for God demands it, that we say: Nevertheless the night is nearly over; the day is almost here. This is what happened at the hour when Jesus was born. Day came.

What is day? Day is the love of God. And the love of God melts away everything that is bad, everything that is sordid, everything that is in despair. Love even vanquishes death. But it has to be a godlike love that loves enemies too; a love that rejects no one and nothing; a love that strides unswervingly through everything, like a hero, and will not be insulted, despised, or rejected; a love that strides through the world with the helmet of hope on its head.

We have not been bold enough in proclaiming this love – that Jesus is born, that all created beings are truly loved. We have not dared for the simple reason that we are too satisfied. It's as if we enjoy being sinners. But in reality no one enjoys being a sinner. Everyone groans under the weight of their sin. Every dying person is hurting and sighing.

God's love strides boldly among us sinners, who are groaning in death. God's love, which became totally human, is poured out into our hearts. Jesus wants us and all people to know that he is the boundless love of God. With this love he wants to be the flame by which we are purified. For it is love alone that receives us into his judgment. It is love that wants to free us from everything that enslaves us and makes us unhappy.

Let us thank the Father in heaven that in Jesus the day has come. Let the day – already at hand – be manifested in your life. Fight for resurrection and life, even if you find yourself in terrible trouble, fear, and distress. With thankfulness in your heart, let the light of God's love pour forth the rays of a new day.

Christoph Friedrich Blumhardt

The Hope That Is Ours

✦   ✦   ✦

49

Fighting to Live

When you were slaves to sin, you were free from the control of righteousness.

What benefit did you reap at that time from the things you are now ashamed of? Those things result in death! . . . For the wages of sin is death, but the gift of God is eternal life in Christ Jesus our Lord. Romans 6:20–21, 23

WHEN IT COMES TO DEATH, we are not dealing with just a sick organism. Human skills can help here or there, and it is our task to do the best we can, as a gardener does his utmost to ensure that his plants are not destroyed. But people who think no further than this do not understand sickness or death. Sickness is part of the work of death, and death is ultimately a consequence of sin.

Destruction of any kind is disorder. It does not belong to life. There is nothing natural about sickness, nothing beneficial; it is something oppressive and contrary to life. Death in the last analysis is a punishment, a punitive power. It is an enemy – indeed, the last enemy!

This is why Jesus calls his church to fight the forces of death. It is no wonder that nursing homes and hospitals originate in the Christian community. We dare not give up on those who are sick and dying. A doctor I met once was very happy about the help in medical science. This made me happy, for it belongs to our human dignity and calling to nurture life. Jesus did not say, "Don't bother about what happens to your life." No, he calls himself the resurrection and the life. "The one who believes in me will live, even though they die" (John 11:25).

Therefore, live and resist the spirit of death. Take courage, no matter how much you have to suffer. Protest against death. It is your human task to live! The judgment against our life is now lifted through Christ. Through him everlasting life can flow into us, and we can overcome our fallen existence. This temporal life, cursed by death, need no longer play the tyrant.

In our earthly existence we poor humans have to journey through the land of death. We are sprayed with its poison from all sides. But Jesus wants to bring us safely through all the regions of death, all the paths on which we can easily become fearful, especially when we are slandered and persecuted by those who do not understand. Dear friends, let us be real fighters, fighters on whom Jesus can lay something without fear of being misunderstood. Christ is the first and the last, who died and came to life. Hold on to this, my dear friends: the Savior died and came to life again, and you will too!

Christoph Friedrich Blumhardt

50

New Victories Ahead

But very truly I tell you, it is for your good that I am going away. Unless I go away, the Advocate will not come to you.

John 16:7

JESUS had to go away to his Father in heaven, away from his disciples who had trustingly left everything to follow him. He had to go away, otherwise he could not send them their true helper, the Holy Spirit. If we think about this a bit, we realize that it was more important for the disciples to receive the "Advocate" than to further their personal relationship with Jesus. In order to become what God had in mind, they had to do without their Lord.

And this is true for us as well. Personal contact with Jesus is wonderful, but we can't depend solely on him to move our hearts. Paul wrote that he would rather die in order to be with Christ, but he realized he needed to remain and work for the brothers (Phil. 1:23–24). When things get hard, too many of us want to fly to heaven, but we are thinking only of ourselves, not of what still needs to be done for the Lord and his kingdom.

To be home with Christ is not the most important thing. We must be ready, right where we are, to fight and bring the joyful news of Christ to the nations. We must pray for new strength in our weakness, for new vigor in sickness, and for new victories in temptation rather than wanting to give up and go to be with the Lord. For it is just in our weakness that the Lord is most powerful (2 Cor. 12:7–10). Hence, even the smallest thing we do can have great significance. One day we will be amazed at how highly the Lord values the faithfulness of his people, especially in their weakness.

Therefore let us not hasten away too soon from here with all our longings but rather pray for a time of grace, for work, and also for much strength from above. Let us do this as much as possible, without resisting the Lord. Then, when the time comes for us to depart, we will be all the more joyfully ready to go be with the Lord.

Johann Christoph Blumhardt

51

Satan's Power Is Broken

On a Sabbath Jesus was teaching in one of the synagogues, and a woman was there who had been crippled by a spirit for eighteen years. She was bent over and could not straighten up at all. When Jesus saw her, he called her forward and said to her, "Woman, you are set free from your infirmity." Then he put his hands on her, and immediately she straightened up and praised God.

Indignant because Jesus had healed on the Sabbath, the synagogue leader said to the people, "There are six days for work. So come and be healed on those days, not on the Sabbath."

The Lord answered him, "You hypocrites! Doesn't each of you on the Sabbath untie your ox or donkey from the stall and lead it out to give it water? Then should not this woman, a daughter of Abraham, whom Satan has kept bound for eighteen long years, be set free on the Sabbath day from what bound her?"

When he said this, all his opponents were humiliated, but the people were delighted with all the wonderful things he was doing. Luke 13:10 –17

WE READ here of a woman who walked in a stooped condition. She was so bent over that she could scarcely look up. Luke says that her infirmity came from a spirit of sickness in which Satan had kept her bound for eighteen long years.

It's amazing that Satan can play such a direct part in a bent body. Does Satan's power reach as far as this? Is it possible that the prince of darkness plays such an active part in something we otherwise would understand in natural terms? Yes. And we must try and grasp better how far the authority of darkness can extend. This question alone, dear friends, is enough to alarm us. But we must not forget the One who crushed the head of the serpent and stands victorious over Satan. He also appears in our text. Therefore, we need not limit ourselves to the gloomy domain of darkness. Indeed, we have every reason to praise the One who has freed us from darkness and led us into light.

Scripture tells us that the power of death belongs to the devil (Heb. 2:14–15); he is "a murderer from the beginning" (John 8:44). The devil clearly has a hand in death. Who sent the great wind that shattered the house that buried the children of Job? Who afflicted Job with loathsome sores? Does this not reveal the power of Satan? Satan indeed still plays his part in bodily infirmities.

Death was not part of God's original plan, nor was sickness, which causes death. Sickness is just the beginning of death. One can almost say that with each new illness something in us dies. Sickness kills a person bit by bit, robbing him of one faculty after another until, in the end, the last flicker of life departs. Little by little, the spirit of death brings us to the grave, even if we are not dogged by any particular illness.

Oh, dear ones, we must surely sigh over all the decay that riddles our world. Not until we experience God's redemption can we truly see the abyss at our feet. Not until we are struck dumb by everything that is required of us – ensnared as we are in so many different hellish bonds – can we see God's glory at work. God's mercy protects us from being fully aware of the condition we are in. Even Scripture only hints at how pervasive the spirit of darkness is so that we do not lose courage and become desolate. Jesus Christ came to destroy the devil's work (1 John 3:8). We must always hold on to this.

✦   ✦   ✦

Our gospel text shows us that Jesus is able to break Satanic bonds. He laid his hands on the woman and said, "Woman, you are set free from your infirmity." This, as indeed everything that the Lord did for sick and bound people, demonstrated that he was the Promised One who could trample on snakes (Luke 10:19).

Who is this Jesus? Who was he? By his steadfast resistance Jesus discredited the powers of darkness completely. Satan tried his hardest with Jesus, torturing him until blood ran, and finally, through his servants, nailing him to the cross. But with patience and with faith in his heavenly Father, Jesus overcame Satan. "He was pierced for our transgressions, he was crushed for our iniquities; the punishment that brought us peace was on him, and by his wounds we are healed" (Isa. 53:5). Yes, healed!

Because of the cross, Satan can no longer bind people in the same way as before. This is why, when he attacks us, we can resist and conquer him in the power of Christ. Whoever fights against the spirit of darkness with faith and determination can be made free of death's sting. The victory is won.

Our Lord now sits at the right hand of God and has received gifts to bestow on us. He fights from above and will do so until he has made his enemies his footstool; until all those spirits of sickness and all those powers that deform or destroy us, whether in body or soul, are removed. Until all of creation, all heaven, and all earth can rejoice. Oh, who can conceive the magnitude of this victory, which we inherit as soon as we believe in Jesus and his victory!

Johann Christoph Blumhardt

52

What Prison Can Hold You?

But we have this treasure in jars of clay to show that this all-surpassing power is from God and not from us. We are hard pressed on every side, but not crushed; perplexed, but not in despair; persecuted, but not abandoned; struck down, but not destroyed. We always carry around in our body the death of Jesus, so that the life of Jesus may also be revealed in our body. For we who are alive are always being given over to death for Jesus' sake, so that his life may also be revealed in our mortal body. So then, death is at work in us, but life is at work in you.

2 Corinthians 4:7–12

GOD NEEDS FIGHTERS who will go through thick and thin for his kingdom. He needs people whose spirits are in heaven, even if while on earth their lives are sorely afflicted and subjected to all kinds of torment. Does God want to plague us? No, not at all, he wants to use us – use us as soldiers to reveal the life of Jesus here on earth.

When you suffer tribulation, keep in mind that you must do so in such a way that it is not just a victory for yourself but a victory over suffering in general. This is what I have experienced among epileptics, among the blind, the lame, and the deaf, and in general among the so-called incurably sick. I tell them: Be glad that you are like this. Now bring something of Jesus' death and his resurrection into your situation, into your trial, your need, your death, into the realm of the incurable which we still see ahead of us. Bring something of Christ into your situation. Then you will help to gain a victory for the whole world.

To express it bluntly, if no one is willing to suffer sickness, if nobody is willing to take on the pangs of death for Christ, how can we ever be victorious over death? If we are always groaning and sullen because we are not as healthy as we would like to be, then what use are we to God? How can the life of Jesus be revealed in our body?

All of us will have to go the way of death, but we can also go the way of resurrection. Submit to death therefore, even if something in you seems to be shattered forever. Let it be shattered. But do not fear, even if you suffer in spirit and have to realize how weak you are. The Risen One can so permeate your weakness that you can be more alive than many proud people who, with all their health and strength, blithely and proudly prance through life.

When you have to bear sickness, especially one that is humanly incurable, stand still, reflect, and remember the One who died and came to life. Rejoice! Make use of your imprisonment and call out to the Lord in faith. Then he will stand by you. Then you will be happier in your prison than all the others who walk the streets in good health.

Ah, dear friends, the Savior wants to help us in all the vicissitudes of life. Remember, our tribulation lasts for only "ten days" (Rev. 2:10), that is, for a short time. Even though you may be in peril of your life, be faithful. Then you will receive the power of life, not only in the sense that you yourself will live, but you will have strength, right where you are, to serve life beyond yourself. Your faithfulness will indeed have eternal significance.

Christoph Friedrich Blumhardt

53

Facing Eternity

Therefore we do not lose heart. Though outwardly we are wasting away, yet inwardly we are being renewed day by day. For our light and momentary troubles are achieving for us an eternal glory that far outweighs them all. So we fix our eyes not on what is seen, but on what is unseen, since what is seen is temporary, but what is unseen is eternal.   2 Corinthians 4:16 –18

YOU ARE GOING toward heaven, to the Savior. Compared to many others who remain in this world full of woe and tears – even if they are healthy – you are to be envied. Meanwhile, take full advantage of your inheritance in heaven while you still have life here on earth. Don't become morose and sad, but be joyful in the Lord, who loves you into all eternity. Be grateful and thank him that he has prepared your soul and made you ready.

It may be that you will have to endure your suffering a bit longer. You may be fearful that your struggle might become harder and more painful. But don't worry. Fix your eyes not on what is seen, but on what is unseen. Learn to take one day at a time, just as a little child would do, who thinks only of the next moment and does not worry about anything else. Compared to eternity, your trials are light and momentary. You have to become completely like a child. That is what the Savior wants, for he can use only children.

Please think deeply about this. Try to become nothing, be a sinner, and seek only his grace. This alone will cancel the debts which could still be held against you. If you submerge yourself completely into his grace, you will find abiding joy. Even the smallest obstacles will come to light and be removed. This will ease your pain, and do you lots of good. Then you will be able to say to your Savior, "You are so good." Entrust everything to the silent rule of the Holy Spirit, who can speak better than you or I. Believe it, God's goal for you is a victorious homecoming.

Johann Christoph Blumhardt

54

You Still Have a Task

*Therefore we are always confident and know that as
long as we are at home in the body we are away from the
Lord. For we live by faith, not by sight. We are confident,
I say, and would prefer to be away from the body and at
home with the Lord. So we make it our goal to please him,
whether we are at home in the body or away from it.*

2 Corinthians 5:6–9

E V E R Y O N E must get to the point where they
come to the Savior alone in peace and quiet,
where they can turn their eyes ever more trustingly toward him, in order that, when the hour of
parting is at hand, union with him will be serene and
untroubled. Jesus always comes closer the more we are
able to let go of the things of this world, when we learn
to accept everything quietly.

As long as we are at home in the body, we must make it
our concern that the Savior may soon have mercy on all
human suffering, whether or not we live to see it – even

if this means more work for us. Therefore, allow yourself to become a poor soul whose focus is on the coming of the Lord, one who sighs with compassion, longing for the Savior to change all things soon. When you can give yourself to this, you have a wonderful task. Your sighs will not be in vain. This will also prepare you for a place in heaven, enabling you to help with whatever your tasks will be there. You surely will have a task, as long as the Savior still has work to do.

Although you are getting weaker, may you be given the certainty that you belong to the Savior forever. This will comfort you, and in spite of all the hardships you still have to endure, he will give you a holy joy. It is perfectly all right to long for your Savior and to ask him to shorten your suffering, or rather, to prepare you soon so that nothing can impede your victorious homecoming. This is the aim of my prayers for you. The dear Savior, who has given you so much, will do his part and meet you with his mercy. "All things work together for good to those who love God" (Rom. 8:28), and when you get to heaven, you will be surprised how wonderful the ways of the Lord have been.

If you think that you have had little opportunity to serve your Savior, remember that fighters are also needed in eternity, just as Christ himself continues to be an advocate on our behalf (1 John 2:1). You will get your assignment, and you will rejoice in it. Just stand firm and allow everything to be removed from you that might hold you back. The Spirit of God will continue to work in you if you submit willingly to his will. His comfort rests precisely in his fatherly hand. May the grace of God in Christ Jesus rest with you until your last breath.

Johann Christoph Blumhardt

55

God's Love Is Forever

For I am convinced that neither death nor life, neither angels nor demons, neither the present nor the future, nor any powers, neither height nor depth, nor anything else in all creation, will be able to separate us from the love of God that is in Christ Jesus our Lord. Romans 8:38–39

PAUL WRITES that absolutely nothing, whether it be sad, shaking, or puzzling, should cause us to doubt God's love. God's love is firm as a rock and unshakable. Absolutely nothing can separate us from God's love.

The heart of our passage lies in the words, "I am convinced." This sure hope, this unwavering trust in God through Christ, can never be taken away. Through Christ we are certain that nothing can make us doubt God's love. However much tribulation may befall us, the more we suffer with Christ, the more we are his beloved children. To be certain of this, that is faith.

For this reason, whoever knows Christ rightly, especially his cross, can say with Paul, God loves me, whether I live or die. God loves me, even if the angels of Satan or principalities or powers of darkness are against me. God loves me, even if I am attacked by his enemies. God will deal with them when it is the right time. Even so, God loves me. God loves me, whether I suffer tribulation in the present or whether I expect it in the future or whether I am attacked by powers from above or below. No matter what or who wants to harm me or really does harm me, I can hold onto this with certainty: God loves me!

Johann Christoph Blumhardt

56

There Is a Crown of Life

Be faithful, even to the point of death, and I will give you life as your victor's crown. Whoever has ears, let them hear what the Spirit says to the churches. The one who is victorious will not be hurt at all by the second death.

Revelation 2:10 –11

WHEN WE BECOME healthy our best days are over. This is because our difficult days can be turned into fighting days. When we are sick, we have the opportunity to call on the Lord in a special way, to fight alongside him in his suffering. We can stand completely with him against the need of the world. We can cry out, look up to heaven – awake and expectant – and truly pray, "Your kingdom come, your will be done!" (Matt. 6:10). When we do this, we are of far more use to the kingdom than those who happily enjoy good days. Isn't it true that healthy days often produce extremely little – a cheerless heart and a dull spirit? But sick days, if we turn to God, can help to make us and others into citizens of heaven.

The crown of life is already waiting for us – something of eternity can be felt, something of God is made evident on earth. The crown is already there, the good that others feel works ever more powerfully among us. We all know that a baby prince will one day wear a crown. Although he is but a child, his servants bow to him and keep enemies away. In the same way, since we are children of God, we are conquerors who will receive the crown. We are surrounded by God's servants: angels and powers of God who intercede for our protection. And the enemy has to yield.

To experience this we must stay right at Jesus' side. We dare not take a single step unless he goes with us. Without him we cannot remain faithful even for a moment. But with him we can dare to oppose death. That is something very deep and very hard, but we can do it in God's strength. And we must dare it for the sake of others. In all our weakness, God wants us to draw eternal life down into our mortal life, even when in the grip of death. In this way we can help hasten the time when the last enemy will be destroyed.

This way the second death – the pains of death in eternity – cannot harm us. Ah, dear friends, this second death is serious and of grave significance for all of us. But fear not, the Lord will help us stay faithful. It is a promise. And even if we are already seized by death and hell, even if we are imprisoned and so overpowered that we can hardly see the light of life, let us remember that Christ has the last word over all those who cherish his name.

May the Lord bless our life together, may he with his Spirit visit all who are sick, so that they can overcome the evils that beset them and not lose heart.

Ah, dear Savior, give us the crown of life, not for our sake, but for the sake of those who for your glory should also receive life. Give a crown of life to all of us in this poor world who long to be your disciples. Give us more courage, Lord, and let us be more joyful. Let us not despair. Amen.

Christoph Friedrich Blumhardt

57

Death Has No Sting

This grace was given us in Christ Jesus before the beginning of time, but it has now been revealed through the appearing of our Savior, Christ Jesus, who has destroyed death and has brought life and immortality to light through the gospel.   2 Timothy 1:9–10

THROUGH CHRIST death is robbed of its power and we will arise from death through him at his appointed time. It says: "Where, O death, is your victory? Where, O death, is your sting?" (1 Cor. 15:55).

But how was death destroyed, and how were life and immortality *really* brought to light? All of us have to die and all of us will have to endure the terrors of death. So how is it different now? To begin with, for those of us who believe, even though we have to die, death is something different from what it was before we met Jesus. Our Savior says, "The one who believes in me will live, even though they die" (John 11:25). And Revelation says, "Blessed are the dead who die in the Lord" (Rev. 14:13).

When you think about it, no one has actually ever seen death. We only see dying and the decay of the body, but not death. And believe me, there is more to death than dying. If it goes so badly with the body after dying, how will it go with the soul from which the death of the body originates?

In the Old Testament we read about Hades, a world of the dead. The description of it is not a pretty picture. David says, "Among the dead no one proclaims your name. Who praises you from the grave?" (Ps. 6:5). Who knows how much power death had over poor humankind even after death, before Christ came?

But in Christ, things are different now – that is, things are different for those who have accepted the gospel. Indeed, through Christ a complete change in connection with death has occurred. Christ has broken "the power of him who holds the power of death at his command – that is, the devil" (Heb. 2:14). Christ has destroyed death and brought life and immortality.

What then of death? We can say with confidence that those who die in the Lord know death's power only on earth, but not in the world beyond. Indeed, through death, life and immortality come to us. Light comes to us – a heavenly light – precisely when the light on this earth is extinguished. Therefore we can say, "Death, I have nothing to do with you anymore. You can no longer plague and harass me. I am free of you, though I still have to wait for the day of resurrection."

Jesus was put to death in the body, but made alive in the Spirit (1 Pet. 3:18). Death had no further power over him, and death has no power over those who die in Christ, even though we must wait for the day of resurrection. We who belong to the Lord can be joyful when we close our eyes and see the great Victor who has broken death's power. We will see, and those around us will see, how triumphantly the departing soul takes hold of the life to come.

Johann Christoph Blumhardt

58

God Won't Let You Go

About three in the afternoon Jesus cried out in a loud voice, "Eli, Eli, lema sabachthani?" (which means, "My God, my God, why have you forsaken me?").

Matthew 27:46

P R A I S E   G O D   T H A T   J E S U S   passed through the valley of the shadow of death for us! And for him it was gloomier than it could possibly be for any human being. He felt abandoned even by God, and yet in his forsakenness he was still able to cry out, "My God! My God!"

Do you grasp how important it is not to let yourself feel abandoned by our dear Lord in hours of forsakenness? Our Savior cried, "Eli, Eli!" The Hebrew word consists of "El," meaning "God," and "i" meaning "my," which is written as a mere dot or stroke. Yet with this tiny dot Jesus held on to the thread leading to his Father's heart. Think of faith like a grain of mustard seed and remember what we are able to achieve with that, according to the Lord's promise.

In deep anguish Jesus fought his way through to faith. In so doing he became our Savior. Therefore, we must "consider him who endured such opposition from sinners, so that you will not grow weary and lose heart" (Heb. 12:3). Because he came through the valley of death, he can guide us through it too. "Even though I walk through the valley of the shadow of death, I will fear no evil, for you are with me; your rod and your staff, they comfort me" (Ps. 23:4).

Our burdened conscience wants to rob us of his comfort. That can indeed make it hard! And yet, Christ shed his blood for us. Hence even our own bad conscience need no longer take our courage away, as long as we hold on to him. "Your rod and your staff, they comfort me." What a rod and staff Jesus can be for us!

While we are on our pilgrimage here on earth, the path goes constantly through deadly need. Comforted by Jesus' own struggle, let us pursue our road in unruffled tranquility, even though we are harried, tormented, and set upon in many ways. He is our blessed hope (Tit. 2:13). At all cost let us hold on to him, the crucified and risen one. Let us take him as a rod to walk with and a staff to lean on. And go ever onwards. He leads us to the glory of his kingdom.

Johann Christoph Blumhardt

59

God's Promise Prevails

When he had received the drink, Jesus said, "It is finished."
With that, he bowed his head and gave up his spirit.

John 19:30

IN THE BIBLE death is not just a matter of being
transferred into the hereafter. No, death is a spirit,
which enters in when we do not know where to
turn, when we are downcast, despairing. Death comes
to us when we are caught up in the march of time, in the
things of this world, when we cannot see more than the
past, or beyond money, house, and land. This is death.
This is why life's most important question is: Have we
completed our mission on earth? If we have, we can
die joyfully. That is why Jesus said, "It is finished." Not
being finished, well, that is death!

Jesus also said, "Whoever believes in me, he will
not die, even though he meets death. I will make him
whole. I can cancel his shortcomings. I am the resurrection and the life. What I began on earth I will complete

for the cripples and the lame, the blind and the deaf. For anyone who believes in me and lives in me, there is life – growth into eternity. Your hour has come, death is no more!"

Sorrow lies in our failure to become whole. We weep because we drag along so much that is unfinished. But God will wipe away these tears from our eyes. He will forgive our failings, he will make right again whatever is broken and set us on a new footing. What we have not been able to finish, he will complete for us, if this is our true longing. This is the promise of the resurrection. What Adam and Eve did not accomplish in Paradise will be finished and what we have failed to do will be completed. There is always hope.

Christoph Friedrich Blumhardt

60

New Life Coming

He who was seated on the throne said, "I am making
everything new!" Revelation 21:5

THE YEARNING of the whole world reaches
out toward the day when Christ will make
everything new. Yes, everything, without
exception, everything will be made new.

If you want to work for this, you will first have to
hand over your own life. Your life will have to go to the
repair shop, so to speak, even if you are afraid that everything will have to be taken apart like an old machine.
The Bible says, "Everything new!" This means you will
also have to sacrifice what is good – or what seems good
to you – especially what you have grown accustomed to.
Everything has to go to the repair shop.

You must give the whole world over to God, joyfully,
completely, every day, in all circumstances. As long
as you keep back areas of your life – even if they are

good – they will not be made new. You must surrender everything to God before he can make everything new.

And when at last the whole will of God, his good, perfect, gracious will is in your heart, and when God's will on earth corresponds to his will in heaven, then the greatest miracles will come to pass.

Christoph Friedrich Blumhardt

61

I Am with You Always

Remember, I am with you always. I am with you all the days.   Matthew 28:20

AS TIME GOES BY you may become weak and discouraged by the fleeting nature of all that surrounds you. You may not know from one day to the next whether what is dearest to you will remain. It is then that God himself will step in. He is with you. "I am with you always!"

The presence of God is our faith. In it we must live. God is with us, he is close to us; we are never alone. Although your fate appears dark and troubled, even though you are hardly able to see ahead, nevertheless, you are not alone. The Savior has bound you to himself; something new will fill you. A power will come to you – a strength and a hope to triumph over every burden you have to bear.

Each one of us is in a struggle unto death, a painful fight. The question is, "How shall we bear it?" All of us are like a troubled world full of storms and attacks, of deep pain and death pangs. Many times we are hardly able to breathe. Yet rejoice! This daily fight is a daily victory. You will surely find yourself surrounded by great, powerful hosts, and the victory of your Savior will be revealed to you and all those around you.

"I am with you always." Let this word be your strength and watchword! Always! Let the presence of God be alive in you. Rejoice! You are being allowed to experience the good news that God is with you. God is always present – the very power that can redeem all who are open to it.

"I am with you all the days." Which days? We often feel so lonely. Our days get so dark that at times we cannot even think about God. We get discouraged by all the foolish things we have done. Yet even the darkest days are days God has given to you. Remember this. Every day that you have lived belongs to your days. All those years, those hours, those times you spent that seem wasted, all your experiences, all your joys, all that gives you courage for life, all that depresses you, saddens you – all this belongs to your days. But it is into these very days and hours that your dear Savior enters. If some of your days are soiled, he shall clean them. If they are dark, he shall shine his light on them so you may have joy again. In your happy days too, look, he is present. He stands by you every single day. Perhaps you haven't noticed him, yet he has been and is with you through all your days. All your days are in his hand. Your future days too!

When you look back over your life, there may be things of which you are ashamed. Yet, surely Jesus was with you. He penetrates into all your days, even back to the first day of your life (Psalm 139). The redeeming Spirit of Jesus has always been at work in your life, even if much of it has been wrong. God has been with you. He reaches down into all your days! Your whole life has in some way or another been lit up by his presence.

Can you grasp that even now, in your poor, lowly body, you can experience the presence of the Savior? Wherever you are, whatever you can or cannot do, you can always represent the Savior. All your fighting and living, all your pain and your victories, can give witness to the Savior. When you receive comfort, the whole world is comforted. When your sins are forgiven, there is hope for the whole world. When you overcome the throes of sickness and death, then the Savior's mercy extends out to many, many people. "Remember, I am with you always, I am with you all the days." This is the gospel.

Somewhere in this world the darkness – the suffering, the chains and fetters that bind people – must be broken. Perhaps you have been chosen to be bound so that the fetters that bind so many other people may be broken. Maybe it's your turn to be downcast. Remember, the comfort you receive can comfort others. Or maybe death is at your doorstep – even then the hope of resurrection can be revealed through you. In all this, God himself will come to you – Jesus will draw close to you quite personally. He has bound himself to you, come what may.

Therefore, do not be afraid! Whatever your struggle, and whatever you have to fight through now, even if it is very small, is important for eternity. Jesus' power can work through you and flow out to others. Remain a willing servant. Then you will bear the stamp of his work.

All the long hours of waiting, all that weighs you down and torments you, all the dark powers you don't understand but often sense, all the restlessness – all this will come to an end! Eternity will surely draw close to you. God himself will lift you out of all the chance happenings of time, all that is not from him, and into his very presence. Eternal powers of love will come very quietly, and when they do you will hardly be able to imagine how great these powers of God are. A new world will lie before your very eyes.

Christoph Friedrich Blumhardt

Further Reading

The Awakening:
One Man's Battle with Darkness
Friedrich Zündel

A gripping account of Johann Christoph Blumhardt's epic prayer battle and the revival that followed.

Action in Waiting
Christoph Friedrich Blumhardt

In these essays, Blumhardt points us to active expectation of God's kingdom here on earth.

Evening Prayers:
For Every Day of the Year
Christoph Friedrich Blumhardt

These faith-filled prayers will help you turn to God and feel his nearness at the end of every day.

Now Is Eternity:
Comfort and Wisdom for Difficult Hours
Christoph Friedrich and
Johann Christoph Blumhardt

Comforting words of wisdom for life's difficult hours, from father and son Blumhardt.

Be Not Afraid:
Overcoming the Fear of Death
Johann Christoph Arnold

Stories of ordinary men, women, and children who found
strength to conquer their deepest fears.

Cries from the Heart:
Stories of Struggle and Hope
Johann Christoph Arnold

True stories of men and women who overcame incredible
adversity through prayer.

Rich in Years:
Finding Peace and Purpose in a Long Life
Johann Christoph Arnold

Why shouldn't growing older be rewarding? These stories
show that despite the trials that come with aging, life can
take on new depth of meaning and purpose.

Plough Publishing House
www.plough.com or e-mail: info@plough.com

PO BOX 398, Walden, NY 12586, USA
Brightling Rd, Robertsbridge, East Sussex, TN32 5DR UK
4188 Gwydir Highway, Elsmore NSW 2360 AUSTRALIA

Sources

Blumhardt, Christoph Friedrich. *Christoph Blumhardt: Eine Auswahl aus seinen Predigten, Andachten und Schriften.* Edited by R. Lejeune. 4 vols. Zürich: Rotapfel Verlag, 1925–32.

_____ *Hausandachten für alle Tage des Jahres.* Berlin: Furche Verlag, 1926.

_____ *Vom Reich Gottes.* Edited by Eugen Jäckh. Berlin: Furche Verlag, 1925.

_____ *Von der Nachfolge Jesu Christi.* Edited by Eugen Jäckh. Berlin: Furche Verlag, 1923.

Blumhardt, Johann Christoph. *Gesammelte Werke: Schriften, Verkündigung, Briefe.* Edited by Paul Ernst, Joachim Scharfenberg, Gerhard Schäfer, and Dieter Ising. 14 vols. Göttingen: Vandenhoeck & Ruprecht, 1968–2001.

9 780874 867961